P9-CBT-061

THE PROCESS OF OPPOSITION IN INDIA

Robert W. Stern

THE PROCESS
OF OPPOSITION IN
INDIA Two Case Studies
of How Policy
Shapes Politics

The University of Chicago Press
Chicago and London

International Standard Book Number: 0–226–77314–0
Library of Congress Catalog Card Number: 78–116029

THE UNIVERSITY OF CHICAGO PRESS, CHICAGO 60637
THE UNIVERSITY OF CHICAGO PRESS, LTD., LONDON

To my mother and father

Surely the churning of milk
bringeth forth butter
Prov. 30:33

Contents

Acknowledgments

To the people who were kind enough to submit to my interviewing and patient enough to answer my many questions and to help me to ferret out material that was frequently tucked away in nooks and crannies, I owe a particular debt of gratitude. Without their cooperation I could not have done my work. My friend and colleague S. P. Nirash helped me in countless ways to bridge the gap of understanding between his culture and mine, and for these services I am heavily in his debt.

Paul Brass, Dennis Dalton, Howard Erdman, Marcus Franda, D. Joy Humes, George Kraft, and Lloyd and Susanne Rudolph either discussed my work with me or read parts of the manuscript. Their assistance helped me to clarify my ideas and undoubtedly saved me from even greater errors than those that I may have committed. Henry Hart lit the candles and helped with the sandwiches all along the way; my debts to him are heavy and long standing.

The American Institute of Indian Studies provided the funds which made this book possible and the Institute's staff in India, particularly D. D. Karve and P. Mehendiratta, was a source of many kindnesses. Wells College provided some additional research funds, time and encouragement to do my work, and an academic environment conducive to scholarly inquiry.

1

THE PROCESS
OF OPPOSITION

This book comprises two studies of the process of opposition in Indian politics or, more exactly, of the process of successful opposition at the national level of Indian politics. They were made in an attempt to reconcile two observations about national politics in India that are both commonplace and apparently contradictory.

The first observation is that the Congress party has been the Indian political system's "one dominant party." This concept of "one-party dominance" was formulated in an attempt to differentiate democratic systems such as India's from those of the more familiar "one-party" authoritarianisms. As applied to India, these terms appeared initially in the works of Professors Rajni Kothari and W. H. Morris-Jones,[1] and they have since been used generally in the literature of comparative politics to describe India's political system, at least until recently.

For twenty years, from the time of Independence until the fourth general elections in 1967, Congress party ministries, sustained by persistent and sufficiently disciplined parliamentary majorities, enjoyed virtually uninterrupted tenure in New Delhi and in the legislative assemblies in almost all the states of the Indian Union. Across the aisles from the treasury benches, opposition parties, numerically weak and fragmented into a variety of mutually antagonistic groups, demonstrated a general inability, either singly or in any combination, to provide the system with any alternative group of rule-makers.[2] The results of the fourth general elections and their

1. Rajni Kothari, "The Congress 'System' in India," *Asian Survey* 4 (December 1964): 1164–73, and W. H. Morris-Jones, *The Government and Politics of India* (London: Hutchinson and Co., 1964).
2. There have been exceptions. For a list of these see Myron Weiner, "Political Development in the Indian States," in *State Politics in India*, edited by Myron Weiner (Princeton, N.J.: Princeton University Press, 1968). The most persistent exception has been Kerala, where Congress has never gained a parliamentary majority and where in 1957 a Communist government came to power

1

aftermath of ministerial instability in states with non-Congress coalition governments suggest the continuation of this general inability
no less than a dimunition of Congress's "dominant" position.

The second observation, equally commonplace, is that Congress,
for all its "dominance" has frequently retreated in the face of opposition; and opposition parties, for all their weaknesses, have not been
ineffective in the charge. Professors Kothari and Morris-Jones agree
that opposition parties in India have exerted an influence on the political system that is out of proportion to both their parliamentary
strength and their willingness to work together.[3]

It may be possible to take a first step toward reconciling these
paradoxical observations by making a distinction between the functioning of opposition parties and the process of opposition. Opposition parties function as part of the oppositional process, and in this
process they have played varying, although not necessarily direct-
ing, roles. Indian society and the Indian political system, including
opposition parties and Congress groups, however, have considerable latent capacity to articulate oppositional inputs, at least inter-
mittently, and to compel decision makers to take them seriously.

The great number and variety of primordial, subnational, and
economic groups which make up the intricate, irregular, and changing weave of Indian society have been major producers of oppositional inputs. Modern means of transportation and communication
have facilitated the mobilization of these groups for political action,
and the receptivity of democratic governments to pressure from organized groups has given this mobilization impetus.[4] Local caste
groups for example, have been "stretched," to use M. N. Srinivas's

and ruled for more than two years. A faction of the same group, now the Communist Party-Marxist, returned to power as a result of the 1967 general elections as the dominant partner in a coalition of opposition parties, and ruled for
almost three years. The same can be said, however, of only one other "united
front" state government, in Orissa, of the eight that were formed in the
months following February 1967; Paul Wallace, "India: The Dispersion of Political Power," *Asian Survey* vol. 8, February 1968.

3. Kothari, "The Congress 'System'"; and Morris-Jones, *Government
and Politics.* For some examples of opposition party successes see Myron Weiner, *The Politics of Scarcity* (Chicago: University of Chicago Press, 1962).

4. The most significant research in this area has been done by Lloyd I. Rudolph and Susanne H. Rudolph, particularly their "The Political Role of India's Caste Associations," *Pacific Affairs*, vol. 33, March 1962, and Lloyd I.
Rudolph, "The Modernity of Tradition: The Democratic Incarnation of Caste
in India," *American Political Science Review*, vol. 54, December 1965.

metaphor,[5] into caste associations and federations, regional political parties, and blocs within state Congress. All are concerned with securing secular benefits for their members, including those which political power and influence can obtain. The "dominance" of local Congress units, whose sum approximates the "dominance" of the national party, is not infrequently dependent upon their coming to terms with these groups.

Myron Weiner, in describing the opposition of wealthy farmers to Congress's now all-but-forgotten resolution of 1959 calling for the reorganization of agriculture on the pattern of cooperative joint farming, puts it aptly: "Paradoxically the distribution of local power which provides so much strength for the Congress party and ultimately for stable government in the center is a bottleneck for structural changes in rural areas advocated by many national leaders." [6]

Peasants and other groups confront a political system whose aspirations to direct Indian society far exceed its capabilities. Under these circumstances noncompliance is a potent oppositional input.[7] Although Congress has controlled the ministries, the capabilities of these ministries to make enforceable rules, and to penetrate the society's existing structures with its rules, has been limited. Major oppositional inputs also have come in the form of extraparliamentary "direct action" of either the violent or nonviolent, organized or anomic varieties. For Congress governments there has always been the risk that attempts to enforce their rules in the face of widespread noncompliance or "direct action" may readily become counterproductive. Such attempts consume scarce resources — money, skills, and prestige — which might otherwise be allocated to different tasks; they alienate those whom they seek to mobilize, and they organize opposition where it was nonexistent or inchoate.

Within the political system itself Congress's "dominance" has been inherently tenuous. Although many of their counterparts in other developing countries have relied on cruder and less satisfactory instruments, Congress leaders have realized the capacity of

5. M. N. Srinivas, *Social Change in Modern India* (Bombay: Allied Publishers, 1966), p. 98.
6. Weiner, *Politics of Scarcity*, p. 156.
7. For a brief discussion of the power of peasant noncompliance see Edward Shils, "Opposition in the New States of Asia and Africa," *Government and Opposition*, vol. 1, January 1966. Shils terms the peasantry "the most massive, most powerful opposition in all new states." His discussion is part of a series of articles which appear under the general title of "Opposition Today."

their minority to control by means of parliamentary democracy. In doing so they have had considerable, although by no means complete, success in establishing the norms of parliamentary democracy as the norms for legitimate oppositions. In his discussion of opposition in developing areas, Edward Shils observes that "attempts at *coups d'etat* have happened more frequently in one party regimes than in regimes with open opposition parties." [8] But the democratic game is not without its risks. To accept parlimentary democracy as a vehicle for control is to accept the risks that inhere in democracy as a vehicle for potential challenges to that control: the risks of tolerating opposing interests and opposing groups and the risks of relying on persuasion and the maintenance of common interests as the cement of intraparty unity and discipline. For Congress these risks have been substantial. Unpopular policies have united opposition parties into electoral alliances, for example, and these have effectively challenged Congress at the polls by allocating constituencies among their component parties and confronting Congress with straight-fights. In the three general elections that were held between 1952 and 1962, Congressmen, in general, met opposition candidates in multicorner contests and won their victories by simple pluralities. An increased number of straight-fight challenges from an increased number of opposition coalitions to an increasingly unpopular and disunited Congress are perhaps the best combination of explanations for the precipitous decline in the number of parliamentary and legislative assembly seats won by the ruling party in the fourth general elections. In no general elections has Congress ever won a majority of the votes polled.

As Congress "dominance" has been leavened by the limited capabilities of the Indian political system and the democratic nature of that system, so its political oneness has been qualified by its heterogeniety and its limited cohesiveness. Over the years Congress has evolved more and more into a national coalition of state and local groups with interests of their own. Could one party which strove to dominate the political system in so heterogeneous a society as India's, and chose economic and political development through democratic means as its primary goals, have become otherwise? To make policy is to favor some interests over others. To do this is to erode Congress's discipline and unity. Dissatisfied Congressmen can turn for support or solace to opposition groups and by doing so strengthen

8. Ibid.

them and weaken both Congress's grip on power and its compelling attractiveness to those who seek power.

The approach — and the limitations — of the studies to follow are suggested by this brief exposition. Opposition as a systemically relevant phenomenon is approached here not as a continuous function of opposition parties but rather as an intermittent process performed by several groups, only some of which are opposition parties. By and large, in these studies politics was shaped by policy. The oppositional activities of groups, their relationships with each other, and in many instances the groups themselves, emerged as responses to the policies of Congress-Government elites; policies which were formed after only minimal consultation with the interests affected by them, or after no consultation, or after consultation with senior Congressmen who were accepted as authoritative spokesmen for the interests involved. For many of the groups here responding to these policies or to the responses of other groups was their raison d'etre, and their active lifetimes were coterminous with the policies they opposed. But while they were active they developed tacit or explicit, intended or unintended relationships with each other, and these supportive relationships lay at the heart of the oppositional process.

In these studies conflict between policy and opposition was resolved by the abandonment of policy or its substantial revision to meet opposition demands. Thus, opposition succeeded in India's "one-party dominant" system when it resulted in changes in policy rather than in the replacement of one group of policy makers by another. As Congress-Government elites made policy, so Congress-Government elites, although not necessarily the same ones, aggregated oppositional inputs into alternative courses of action or inaction.

Although the primary concern here is with the process of opposition, that process can be neither analyzed nor understood except within the context of its interaction with the processes of government. In his foreword to the first issue of *Government and Opposition*, Leonard Shapiro stated the orientation of that journal in terms that might be applied to this work:

Our field is "government *and* opposition": we are, in a word, concerned to illuminate the one in the light of the other, in the belief that both elements are always and at all times present, or at any rate potentially present, within any political order; and that illumination of the nature of that

political order must be sought now from one aspect of the political process, and now from the other.[9]

The means of illumination employed here is the "case study." In
the following chapters two cases of successful opposition are
presented and compared. The first and longest is a study of opposition in western India during the 1950s to the national Congress-
Government elite's unwillingness to create one unilingual Gujarati-
speaking state and one unilingual Marathi-speaking state with its
capital at Bombay city. The second, involving relatively small and
dispersed groups rather than large and regionally concentrated
ones, is the case of opposition to the Government of India's attempt
beginning in 1963 to curtail severely the domestic consumption and
saving of gold by means of the Gold Control Rules.

In a departure from the usual pattern in such studies, a departure
suggested by their approach, the cases are not presented as unbro-
ken narratives. Rather, they are arranged to facilitate comparisons
between the participant groups in the two cases and their roles and
relationships in the oppositional processes. The next four chapters
are about the backgrounds of the oppositional processes in both
cases (chapter 2) and the oppositional roles and relationships in
both of interest groups (chapter 3), opposition parties (chapter 4),
and groups of Congressmen (chapter 5). Each chapter is divided
into two parts corresponding to the two cases. A final chapter sums
up the studies' findings.

Both cases are of systemic opposition to the efforts of Congress-
Government elites at economic, political, and social reconstruction.
Even "direct action," and there was a considerable amount of this in
both cases, was used by its organizers to achieve systemic goals. Although it seems unnecessary to argue the importance of this type of
opposition in a developing political system, it may be advisable to
note that it has by no means been the only type. There has been
antisystem opposition in India and conventional opposition to worka-
day government policies. The question of a typology of opposition
will not be raised here, however.

It cannot be claimed that what follows in any way surmounts the
ordinary limitations of the case-study method. The two cases ex-
plore, but hardly exhaust, the range of possibilities even in the type
of opposition they illustrate. For example, structures which have an

9. October 1965.

oppositional function, such as the bureaucracies, the courts, and the "watchdog" committees of Parliament, did not perform that function in these cases. Material in the studies may suggest why they did not. But these would be only suggestions.

What questions have been considered? It seems appropriate to raise them here and assume the obligation of trying to answer them as we go along. For example, if supportive oppositional relationships form in response to Congress-Government policies, then it is necessary to ask initially what these policies were, what state- and nation-building problems they were directed toward, and how and why they became problems. What were the relationships between Congress-Government policies and the opposition they engendered? Whose oxen were being gored, how, and by whom? How do the ways in which Congress-Government policies are made, enforced, defended, and legitimated contribute to their opposition?

What was the nature of these supportive oppositional relationships? Who supported whom, how, and why? What for example, were these interest groups in chapter 3? How were they groups, what were their interests, what and whom did they bring together, what and whom did they separate? In both cases group leadership was primarily urban, and in the case of Bombay reorganization cities were the principal points of contention and arenas of oppositional activity. What effect, if any, did this urban bias have on the articulation of group demands? What oppositional supports did groups provide to other groups, opposition parties, and Congressmen? How did supportive oppositional relationships differ in the two cases, how can these differences be explained, and what effects did these differences have on the oppositional process? What influence did participation in the process of opposition have on internal relationships within groups?

Opposition parties were unanimous in their disapprobation of the Congress-Government's Bombay reorganization formulas and the Government of India's Gold Control Rules. What explains this unanimity among parties which are generally contentious, and what effect, under what circumstances, did this unanimity have on the oppositional process? What was the effect on individual party units, on their internal relations and their relations with sibling and parent units when, as in the case of Bombay reorganization, this unanimity was manifested in agitational-electoral-parliamentary coalitions? What were the cooperative-competitive relations among coalition

components, and among coalitions? In comparison to opposition coalitions, how did less structured but no less unanimous opposition
from non-Congress parties, as in the case of the Gold Control Rules,
enter into the oppositional process? How did opposition parties
draw Congressmen into the process of opposition?

There were any number of Congressmen in western India, some
very strategically located, who defected and became dissidents on
the issue of Bombay reorganization. In that case as well as in the
case of opposition to the Gold Control Rules, there were large
groups of Congressmen who dissented from Congress-Government
policies but remained within Congress discipline. Who were these
dissident and dissenting-but-disciplined Congressmen, what were
their stakes in opposition, and what identities, sympathies, and interests did they share with others in the oppositional process? What
were their contributions to the process of opposition and to the re-
establishment and renovation of Congress "dominance"?

2　BACKGROUND

In confronting the problems of states reorganization and gold control, Congress-Government elites came face to face with legacies from their country's past: inheritances of linguistic-provincialism and a tradition of using gold as an ornament metal and a repository for savings. In this chapter these inheritances are described.

The legacy of linguistic-provincialism was one to which the pre-Independence Congress and its leader, Mahatma Gandhi, had been no small contributors. But post-Independence Congress-Government elites viewed both legacies as encumbrances impeding India's progress toward unity and modernity. Sustained in their judgments by "expert" advice and armed with state power, they attempted to cast them by the wayside. But they were not permitted to do so. The sentiments and interests of millions of Indians are too engaged with legacies from the past, and Congress-Government elites have provided them with a political system whose capacity to respond to opposition exceeds (or exceeded) its capacity to convince or compel. Elite responses to oppositional inputs are presented here in skeleton chronologies to orient the reader to their discussion in detailed fragments below.

A Legacy from Gandhi

In 1916 Mahatma Gandhi spoke to students at Banaras — Indian students learning their lessons in English in preparation for English-speaking careers:

Suppose that we had been receiving, during the past fifty years, education through our vernaculars [i.e., regional languages], what should we have today? We should have today a free India, we should have our educated men, not as if they were foreigners in their own land but speaking to the heart of the nation; they would be working among the poorest of the poor, and whatever they would have gained during the past fifty years would be a heritage for the nation.[1]

Four years later at Nagpur, Gandhi presented a new constitution to the Indian National Congress. It provided for the establishment of Congress's provincial units *not* on the administrative lines drawn by the British, but rather on the explicit basis of Congress-formulated "linguistic provinces." [2] Under Gandhi's leadership Congress was embarking on a revolutionary, mass "noncooperation" movement, and for it to be successful the English-speaking graduates who were to be his lieutenants would have to speak, literally, "to the heart of the nation." Henceforth, and to this day, Congress's jurisdiction would be divided among Pradesh (provincial) Congress Committees (PCCs), each, with only one exception, responsible for a Congress-determined, more-or-less unilingual division of India.[3]

The one exception is the Bombay (city) PCC. It is the one purely urban, and the one bilingual, committee. Marathi and Gujarati are its languages. Two other legacies of the Nagpur Constitution should be noted. First, although the jurisdiction of each PCC was confined to a linguistic area, not all linguistic areas were under the jurisdiction of only one PCC. For example, by 1956 Marhattas other than those in Bombay city were divided among four Marathi PCCs: Maharashtra, Vidarbha (Berar), Nagpur, and Marathwada. Second, the determination of linguistic lines was made by a political organization for political purposes.

From its meeting at Nagpur until virtually the eve of India's In-

1. Quoted in Homer A. Jack, ed., *The Gandhi Reader* (Bloomington: Indiana University Press, 1956), p. 131.
2. *Report of the Thirty-fifth Session of the Indian National Congress held at Nagpur on the 26th, 28th, and 31st December 1920* (Nagpur, 1920).
3. It should be noted that Gandhi did not discover the political potential of linguistic-provincialism. Like the Indian rulers whom they gradually replaced, the British drew their administrative lines with little regard for the linguistic map. As Indian nationalism developed during the nineteenth century, this noncoincidence between linguistic and administrative lines became an issue. One of the major nationalist causes célèbres of the twentieth century was the partition in 1905 of the Bengali-speaking area of the sprawling Bengal Presidency. The partition was ordered by the Viceroy Lord Curzon for what he maintained, with singular insensitivity, were reasons of better administration. In response to the growing militance in the nationalist movement which followed this partition, it was undone in 1911. From that date, a number of British politicians concerned with India, among them Lord Hardinge, Montagu and Chelmsford, and Sir John Simon, argued in favor of the limited use of language as a criterion for the demarcation of provincial boundaries.

dependence, a belief in the rightness of linguistic provinces was an article of the Congress faith. In 1928 a committee of nationalist leaders under the chairmanship of Motilal Nehru, the father of India's first prime minister, concluded that in the democratic India of the future "the main considerations" in the reorganization of provinces "must necessarily be the wishes of the people and the linguistic unity of the areas concerned." [4]

In its election manifesto in 1946, with Independence nearly in sight, the Congress, through its working committee, declared that it stood for "the freedom of each group and territorial area within the nation to develop its own life and culture within the larger framework, and for this purpose such territorial areas or provinces should be constituted, as far as possible, on a linguistic and cultural basis." [5]

Then came Independence. And with Independence the partition of the subcontinent and the long night of communal frenzy: murder, looting, arson, war with Pakistan, and millions of refugees. The Congress elite became a national Congress-Government elite in a maelstrom — a maelstrom that carried vivid reminders of the ties that bind Indians to a host of subnational communities and separate them from other Indians and that brought forewarnings of the difficulties to be encountered in capturing for the nascent Indian Union the loyalties of those so bound and separated. The wisdom of Congress's commitment of almost thirty years to the reorganization of India on linguistic lines was forced open to serious reevaluation.

The Constituent Assembly of India officially began this reevaluation by appointing a Linguistic Provinces Commission under the chairmanship of S. K. Dar, a former judge of the Allahabad High Court, to study and make recommendations on provincial reorganization under post-Independence/Partition circumstances.

"Expert" groups such as the Dar Commission appear and reappear with some frequency in both cases in this study. The adjective "expert" is placed in quotation marks not to disparage the expertise of the men who make up these bodies, generally men of some professional stature who are not Congress party leaders, or their judi-

4. All Parties Conference, 1928, *Report of the Committee Appointed by the Conference to Determine the Principles of the Constitution for India* (All-India Congress Committee, 1928).
5. *Congress Bulletin*, 24 January 1946.

ciousness in collecting and sifting evidence. This is done, rather, to
suggest that one of the major functions performed by such groups is
to provide "expert," that is, nonpartisan, legitimation for decisions
already made by political leaders. This function is well known to
students of politics. With regard to provincial reorganization, the
Constituent Assembly was told by its leading member, Jawaharlal
Nehru, that "first things must come first and the first thing is the
security and stability of India." [6]

The Dar Commission, not surprisingly, concurred. After touring
southern and western India, it warned that "nationalism and sub-
nationalism are two emotional experiences which grow at the expense of each other." It advised against provincial reorganization
until there was greater "national integration," and even then, it emphasized, language "should not be the decisive or even the main
factor." [7]

The politicians' counterpoint to the recommendations of the "experts," another recurring phenomenon, was provided by the report
of the JVP Committee, appointed by the Congress at its Jaipur session in December 1948. The committee was composed of Jawaharlal
Nehru, Vallabhbhai Patel, the two leading figures in the post-Independence Congress-Government elite, and Pattambhi Sitaramayya.
All had been members of the Congress Working Committee when it
announced its 1946 election manifesto. The committee acknowledged that Congress policy in the past had been "clearly in favor of
linguistic provinces," but they confessed that in the past Congress
had not been "faced with the practical application of this principle."

It becomes incumbent upon us, therefore, to view the problem of linguistic provinces in the context of today. That context demands above
everything the consolidation of India and her freedom, the progressive
solution of her economic problems in terms of the masses of her people,
the formation of unity in India and of close cooperation among the various provinces and states in most spheres of activity. It demands, further,
the stern discouragement of communalism, provincialism, and all other
separatist, and disruptive tendencies.

"Taking a broad and practical view," the JVP Committee agreed
with the Dar Commission that the immediate post-Independence/

6. Quoted in Government of India, *Report of the States Reorganization
Commission* (1955), p. 14.
7. Constituent Assembly of India, *Report of the Linguistic Provinces Commission* (1948).

Partition period was not "an opportune time" for the formation of new provinces.[8]

But the politicians' and the "experts'" "opportune time" are not necessarily the same. The JVP Committee did not unequivocally affirm for the Congress the Dar Commission's almost unmitigated hostility to linguistic-provincial reorganization. Rather it held open the possibility of such reorganization, which it seemed in principle to oppose, if agreement could be reached among Pradesh Congress leaders. And it suggested that if such an agreement could be reached in Andhra, where a "direct action" campaign was threatening Congress control, a Telegu-language state might be established. In 1953, after the Congress Working Committee had reported a "general agreement" among the "Andhra Provincial Congress Committee, the Tamil Nad [Madras] Congress Committee, and the Madras [Congress] Government in regard to the formation of Andhra Province," and in the wake of widespread violence following the death through fasting of an ascetic advocate of linguistic-provincialism, Andhra came into being.[9]

The door to linguistic-provincial reorganization could not be shut. At best it could only be hinged so that some exertion and some cooperation among Congressmen with conflicting provincial interests would be necessary to open it. The Congress-Government elite and its "experts" had attempted to close the door on the grounds that state- and nation-building considerations suggested that it be shut. But there are other state- and nation-building considerations. To the Congress-Government elite the maintenance of Congress's "dominant" position in Indian politics has also been a state- and nation-building consideration — one of the highest magnitude. "You know how much hangs on the solidarity in the Congress," wrote Congress President U. N. Dhebar to state party leaders at one of the flash points in the controversy over the reorganization of Bombay state. "It is the only force that stands between chaos and order."[10] Dhebar and his colleagues had good reason to know that the price of "solidarity" was compromise and that "solidarity" so achieved was likely to be amorphous and unstable, but better than "chaos and disorder."

8. *Report of the Linguistic Provinces Committee Appointed by the Jaipur Congress* (New Delhi: Indian National Congress, 1949).

9. Indian National Congress, *Resolutions on States Reorganization, 1920–1956*, resolution of November 1949 (New Delhi, n.d.).

10. *Congress Bulletin*, circular no. 46 (January 1956).

In August 1951, two years after it received the JVP Committee's report and on the eve of India's first general elections, the Congress Working Committee observed that "the Congress in its election manifesto . . . has reiterated its adherence to the principle of the formation of linguistic provinces, regard being had also to other considerations." [11] But in May 1953 in its "instructions" to the States Reorganization Commission, the "expert" body appointed to recommend a readjustment of the hinges after the creation of Andhra, the working committee emphasized the "other considerations."

> Any . . . reorganization should take into consideration . . . not only cultural and linguistic matters but also other important factors, such as the preservation of the unity of India, national security and defense, administrative advantages, financial considerations and the economic progress of each State as well as of the whole nation.[12]

The thorniest problem before the States Reorganization Commission was the future of Bombay state and its major linguistic group, the Marhattas, among whom dissatisfaction with the status quo was organized and vocal. In 1954, Bombay state was a strip about 150 miles wide from the Arabian Sea into the Deccan, stretching from Rajasthan down the western coast of India for 1,300 miles into what is now Mysore. In its northern region, Gujarat, there were eleven and a half million speakers of Gujarati. But to the west of them, in the separate states of Saurashtra and Kutch, more than four and a half million more Gujarati speakers lived. The large central region, Maharashtra, was the home of sixteen million Marhattas, speakers of Marathi. But to the east of them in the Nagpur and Vidarbha (Nag-Vidarbha) divisions of Madhya Pradesh and in the Marathwada area of Hyderabad, there were another eleven million Marathi-speakers. Four million speakers of Kannada lived in its southern tip, but the majority of Kannadigas, eight million, were divided among Mysore, Madras, and Coorg.

Bombay city was the state's capital. It is perhaps the most linguistically heterogeneous urban area in India. The largest single linguistic group in the city, though not a majority — 44 percent according to the 1951 census — speaks Marathi. But there is an economically and politically dominant minority of Gujarati-speakers — about 18 percent in 1951 — and smaller linguistic groups, the largest of which speak Hindi, Urdu and south Indian languages.

11. *Resolutions on States Reorganization, 1920–1956.*
12. Ibid.

The Kannada-speaking minority of Bombay state presented no problem of any consequence to the States Reorganization Commission. In its report it recommended that the Kannada-speaking area of the state be detached and integrated into a new unilingual Mysore. In its award of Bombay territory to Mysore, however, it created a problem of Maharashtra irredenta in the districts of Karwar and Belgaum.

But the major problems before the commission were two. First there was the apparently unanimous demand of the Marhattas in Bombay state and city for Samyukta Maharashtra (United Maharashtra), the integration of *all* Marathi-speakers into *one* unilingual state which would have its capital at Bombay city. Second, there was strenuous opposition to this demand from Nag-Vidarbha, Gujarat, Bombay city, and the national Congress-Government elite.

Ironically, the movement for a Marathi-language province originated not in Bombay but in Nag-Vidarbha. Nagpur was part of the British Central Provinces in 1903 when Vidarbha, having been taken from the nizam of Hyderabad, was added to it. In 1917 the Berar (Vidarbha) PCC, arguing that Vidarbha was being exploited for the benefit of the Central Provinces' Hindi-speaking majority, petitioned the secretary of state for India and the viceroy, Montagu and Chelmsford, to recommend the creation of a Marathi-speaking province in central India. By introducing more self-government into provincial affairs, the Government of India Act of 1935 added to the political strength of the Central Provinces' Hindi-speakers, and by 1938 the demand for a separate Marathi province had spread to the Nagpur PCC. In 1940 the Mahavidarbha Samiti (Greater Vidarbha Committee) was formed under the leadership of one of the area's most prominent Congressmen, Dr. M. S. Aney. The samiti wanted a unilingual Marathi-speaking province, Mahavidarbha, to be carved from the four districts of the Central Provinces' Vidarbha division (Amravati, Akola, Yeotmal, and Buldana) and the four districts of its Nagpur division (Nagpur, Bhandara, Wardha, and Chanda).[13]

The movement for Samyukta Maharashtra, which was to dominate the politics of western India between 1956 and 1960, was late in forming. It had its beginnings at a literary conference in the city of Belgaum in 1946. Later that year the litterateurs gave way to the

13. Madhao Shrihari Aney, *Memorandum Submitted to the States Reorganization Commission* (Yeotmal: Yeotmal District Association, n.d.).

politicians, and the Samyukta Maharashtra Parishad (United Maharashtra Conference) was organized. The parishad, though dominated by Congressmen, was supported by almost every political group in Maharashtra.

In August 1947 the movements for Mahavidarbha and Samyukta Maharashtra joined in an uncertain and qualified alliance called, after the city in which it was signed, the Akola Pact.

The Akola Pact provided for one Maharashtra composed of two autonomous subprovinces, Western Maharashtra and Mahavidarbha. In a separate note, two of the pact's leading signatories, Shankarrao Deo, the president of the parishad and general secretary of the Congress, and Brijlal Biyani, the president of the Vidarbha PCC, agreed that "all efforts should be made for the formation of a separate province of Mahavidarbha" if "for any reason" the subprovincial scheme of the Akola Pact could not be realized.[14]

The Dar Commission, for whom the Akola Pact had been prepared, dismissed it as having been "torn asunder" by the conflicting demands of spokesmen for Maharashtra and Mahavidarbha, and recommended that a united province *not* be formed.[15] The JVP Committee, in effect, supported this recommendation but rendered it negotiable by allowing the formation of a joint province to "depend on the choice of Vidarbha and Nagpur," that is, on the choice of the Congress leaders of Vidarbha and Nagpur.

The pact was mooted in 1950 by the Indian constitution, which made no provision for subprovinces. There is no evidence that the signatories from Marathi-speaking Bombay made "all efforts" or even any efforts to support the formation of Mahavidarbha. Aney, implying a breach of faith, claimed that they "strenuously opposed" it.[16] The parishad, somnolent between 1949 and 1953, was reawakened by the appointment of the States Reorganization Commission and it reached out once more for Nagpur and Vidarbha. In September 1953 a new pact was signed at Nagpur city by Congress leaders from Maharashtra and Nag-Vidarbha. It went far beyond the Akola Pact. The agreement signed at Nagpur was for *one* Marathi-speaking state, Samyukta Maharashtra.

The Nagpur Pact assured Nag-Vidarbha of equitable treatment in Samyukta Maharashtra's allocation of resources, cabinet minis-

14. Texts are reproduced in *Report of the Linguistic Provinces Commission.*
15. Ibid.
16. Aney, *Memorandum.*

tries, government jobs, and educational opportunities. Nagpur city, then the capital of Madhya Pradesh, the Central Provinces' successor state, was promised a second seat of the state's high court and one session annually of its legislative assembly.[17]

Three leading Congressmen from Vidarbha who signed the Akola Pact also signed the Nagpur Pact, as did two Congress ministers in Nagpur.[18] This was a battle won for Samyukta Maharashtra, and a setback for Mahavidarbha. But the "pakka Vidarbhites," as M. S. Aney termed them,[19] didn't sign. The States Reorganization Commission, therefore, was clearly confronted with a demand for Samyukta Maharashtra, on the one hand, and a demand for Mahavidarbha on the other.

The Dar Commission and the JVP Committee emphatically rejected the Samyukta Maharashtra Parishad's claim on Bombay city. Both recommended that, in the event of Bombay's division into linguistic provinces, Bombay city should be established as a separate political unit. The reasons they cited for denying the parishad its most heartfelt claim were many: "expert evidence" which indicated that the "commercial and financial interests of Bombay city and of India as a whole would be affected by a sudden change in the form of the government of Bombay," the "practical unanimity" of "all the non-Maharashtrian evidence . . . that the city of Bombay should . . . in no case . . . be placed under a unilingual Government," the incongruity of making "this multi-lingual, cosmopolitan city the capital of a unilingual province," [20] and the belief that Bombay city's attachment to a linguistic province would mean "its rapid deterioration from its present commanding position" as "the nerve-center of our trade and commerce, and our biggest window to the outside world." [21]

In testimony before the States Reorganization Commission, the parishad once again demanded Bombay city for the capital of Sa-

17. Text reproduced in Samyukta Maharashtra Parishad, *Reorganization of States in India with Particular Reference to the Formation of Maharashtra* (Bombay, 1954). The pact also promised "special attention" to Marathwada, the least developed of the Marathi-speaking areas.

18. Ramrao Deshmukh, Gopalrao Khedkar, Sheshrao Wankhede; R. K. Patil and P. K. Deshmukh.

19. *Free Press Journal*, 28 September 1959.

20. *Report of the Linguistic Provinces Commission*.

21. *Report of the Linguistic Provinces Committee*.

myukta Maharashtra, and once again the same arguments were marshaled against it.

The States Reorganization Commission submitted its report in September 1955. Its recommendations for the reorganization of Bombay can only be termed ingenious. It attempted to give something to everyone and at the same time preserve the status quo. But the Marhattas, who demanded the most, received the least.

The commission recommended that a bilingual, Marathi and Gujarati state be established. A bilingual state, "balanced" between a population that was to be about 46 percent Marathi and 37 percent Gujarati—a slight advantage for the Marhattas, but not enough to frighten the Gujaratis, who had resources other than numbers. The balance was to be struck by incorporating Gujarati-speaking Kutch and Saurashtra and Marathi-speaking Marathwada, *but not Nag-Vidarbha*, into the new state. Keeping Nag-Vidarbha separate from Bombay by creating Mahavidarbha would serve both to maintain the "balance" in Bombay and to meet the demands of the Nagpur and Vidarbha PCCs' separatists. Bombay city would not be taken from the Maharashtrians, but it would not be placed under their sole control either—a control to which the Gujarat PCC, the Gujarati-dominated Bombay PCC, and the Congress-Government elite objected.[22]

The Maharashtra PCC rejected "balanced bilingual" Bombay out of hand, as did the Samyukta Maharashtra Parishad and all the opposition parties which were members of the parishad. Citing "the opinion expressed by the Maharashtra Pradesh Congress Committee," the Congress Working Committee decided in October 1955 "not to press for the acceptance of the recommendation of the States Reorganization Commission in favour of a composite State of Bombay."[23] Between October 1955 and the passage of the States Reorganization Act by Parliament in August 1956, the Congress-Government elite and provincial Congress leaders tried to renegotiate a settlement of the Bombay reorganization question. These negotiations took place within the context of mounting pressure on the Congress "system" from outside and increasing disaffection within.

In October 1955, the Maharashtra PCC, acting without the ap-

22. *Report of the States Reorganization Commission*, pp. 112–25.
23. November 1955, *Resolutions on States Reorganization, 1920–1956*.

proval of its Samyukta Maharashtra Parishad allies, suggested to the working committee, as an alternative to "balanced bilingual" Bombay, "big bilingual" Bombay; that is, one state composed of all Gujarati and Marathi-speaking areas, including Nag-Vidarbha. To this proposal the Maharashtra PCC added a crucial and controversial provision that Gujarat, if it wished, could exercise an "option" to leave the composite state after five years.

"Balanced bilingual" Bombay was acceptable to the Gujarat PCC. But it immediately rejected the proposal for a "big bilingual" state, a state in which an overwhelming Marhatta majority might very well compel the Gujaratis to exercise their "option," leaving Bombay city behind them. Instead, the Gujarat PCC resolved itself in favor of a "three-unit" solution; the establishment of Maharashtra, Gujarat, and Bombay city as separate political units, as an alternative to the States Reorganization Commission's recommendation. The renegotiations among Congress hierarchs that followed the development of this impasse were a search for a "three-unit" formula that would be acceptable to Maharashtra. The Maharashtra PCC bargained for an assurance that Bombay city's tenure as a separate unit would be only temporary, but the "three-unit" scheme that was initially incorporated into the States Reorganization Bill of 1956 included no such guarantee.

When the bill in this form came to a vote in Parliament in August 1956, an ad hoc multiparty group of M.P.s including leaders of the Bombay PCC pressed the government to withdraw the "three-unit" provision in favor of a "big bilingual" scheme which would not include a quit "option" for Gujarat. The government acceded to this demand and the bill was passed in the Lok Sabha (the lower house) by a vote of 241 to 40. "Big bilingual" Bombay became a state in the Indian Union on 1 November.

Nothing was really settled. The creation of the "big bilingual" state was greeted by the eruption of a linguistic-provincial opposition movement in hitherto quiescent Gujarat. Among the Marhattas the demand for Samyukta Maharashtra continued unabated, and dissatisfaction in Nag-Vidarbha increased. Buffeted by defeats at the polls, dissidence, violence, and the prospect of things getting worse rather than better, the Congress-Government elite opened a second series of renegotiations in August 1959 for the purpose of bifurcating "big bilingual" Bombay. The Bombay Reorganization Act of 1960 was passed by Parliament in April and the new unilingual states of Gujarat and of Maharashtra, with its capital at Bombay city, came into being in May.

A Legacy from Sita

The wedding costumes of Sita, the bride of Rama, and the three other brides of King Dasharatha's sons are described in the Sanskrit epic *Ramayana*.

Crimson bridal robes, woven with gold, shimmered on each fair form. Their slender arms were loaded with bangles of gold and gems, and five diamond finger rings on each hand were chained by gems to a jewelled lotus bracelet. Seven strands of matchless pearls and a bridal garland of jasmine flowers adorned each fair maid. Silver anklets with tiny bells tinkled on little feet, bordered with crimson lac, and lustrous pearls swung from shapely ears. A dazzling diadem was placed on each royal brow, and a gossamer veil of gold and silver enfolded each radiant bride.[24]

In the centuries that separate Sita from the daughters of contemporary wealth, bridal fashions have changed little. But the builders of modern India have not been dazzled by the gorgeous display. Mahatma Gandhi's reflections on his own wedding contrast sharply with the description of Rama's.

Marriage among Hindus is no simple matter. The parents of the bride and the bridegroom often bring themselves to ruin over it. They waste their substance, they waste their time. Months are taken up over the preparations — in making clothes and ornaments and in preparing budgets for dinners. Each tries to outdo the other in the number and variety of courses to be prepared. Women whether they have a voice or no, sing themselves hoarse, even get ill, and disturb the peace of their neighbors. These in turn quietly put up with all the turmoil and bustle, all the dirt and filth, representing the remains of the feasts, because they know that a time will come when they also will be behaving in the same manner.[25]

One of the ways in which the parents of the bride have traditionally brought "themselves to ruin" has been through supplying their daughters with a dowry of gold jewelry. Wedding ceremonies are a major occasion for the purchase of gold. And Gandhi objected to this too. Even when he was still in South Africa, at the beginning of his political career, he "was exhorting people to conquer the infat-

24. Translated by Shudha Mazumdar (Bombay: Bharatiya Vidya Bhavan, 1953).
25. *Autobiography* (Ahmadabad: Navajivan Publishing House, 1927).

uation for jewellery," and on one occasion he persuaded his wife to return an expensive gift from local Indians, a necklace "worth fifty Guineas," in spite of her accusation that he was unfairly penalizing his children and adversely affecting their marriage prospects.[26]

In announcing the Gold Control Rules' restrictions on the manufacture and sale of gold jewelry, Finance Minister Morarji Desai, a man in the Gandhian mold, addressed himself to the relief of Indian parents.

> I have no doubt that most families in India will welcome [the rules] with a real sense of relief. . . . Nine out of ten families which buy ornaments in our country are obliged to do so under social pressure and at great cost and inconvenience to them.[27]

To the anthropologist M. N. Srinivas, the Gold Control Rules of 1963 were a supplement to the Dowry Prohibition Act of 1961. According to Srinivas it is customary among upper and trading castes for the bride to bring a minimum of gold jewelry when she is given in marriage. The higher the groom's family's position, the more is expected. "Custom demands that the groom's family be rapacious and extract as much . . . gold as possible from the bride's people." [28]

In its most elegant and elaborated forms, Indian gold jewelry rivals the best goldsmith's handiwork produced anywhere in the world.[29] But gold jewelry is valued in India not only for its beauty. For many Indians it has, in addition, symbolic and economic significance, and for almost all Indians gold has traditionally meant only "pure gold"; that is, gold of a fineness of about twenty carats or above. Until recently, the fourteen-carat gold common in Western ornaments has been associated in India with nothing grander than fountain pen points. It is important to note this. The Gold Control Rules were directed specifically against the consumption of "pure gold."

"Pure gold" ornaments which are given in connection with wed-

26. Ibid.
27. *Statesman*, 10 January 1963.
28. "Attachment to Gold," *Hitavada*, 25 February 1963.
29. The reader who has never seen any actual pieces is enthusiastically referred to the illustrations in Jamila Brij Bhushan's *Indian Jewellery, Ornaments, and Decorative Designs* (Bombay: D. B. Taraporevala and Sons, 1964), and in the issue of *Marg: A Magazine of the Arts*, Bombay, September 1964, devoted to Indian jewelry.

ding ceremonies are for many Indians a symbol of the sacredness of marriage. The wedding necklace of south India, "the Sacred Mangalyan," according to a group of goldsmiths who make them, requires "pure fresh gold which has been melted on an auspicious occasion." [30] This attachment to "pure gold" as a marriage symbol is reinforced by the fashion preference of Indian women who are no longer brides. They complain that fourteen-carat gold is unsuitable to the Indian climate — that it stains their skins and turns color.[31] In India, as elsewhere, expensive jewelry is symbolic of high class status. Customarily, it is also symbolic of high caste status. Hutton quotes eight prohibitions propounded in 1930 by the Kallar, a caste in Tamilnad, against certain types of behavior among local untouchables. The first of these is "that the Adi-Dravidas shall not wear ornaments of gold and silver." [32]

According to the ancient *Laws of Manu*, the ornaments given to a woman by her husband and relatives at the time of her wedding are *stridhana* — her separate property. Theoretically, this is an important source of personal security for her in a society in which widows generally have had no claim on the real property left by their husbands. But more likely, the bride's jewelry will become part of her family's savings, to be supplemented as family surpluses are converted into additional ornaments or hoarded in the form of bullion and to be depleted as unforeseen contingencies or heavy expenses, such as her daughters' weddings, are met.

"Pure gold" is also preferred for savings. It is customary and economical. The advantages of gold are that it is easily concealed, easily portable, and highly liquid. Why pay the goldsmith or jeweler the same or higher charges for making ornaments of lesser value, for diluting precious metal with worthless alloys? Gold was used as a "domestic bank" during centuries of endemic political turmoil and long before the establishment of institutions for savings. Insofar as these conditions persist, gold remains a wise investment. Millions of

30. Tamilaha Viswakarma Central Sangam, Madras, *Memorandum Submitted to the Joint Committee of Parliament on the Gold (Control) Bill, 1963* (mimeographed, n.d.). See also, S. Narayanaswamy, "Gold and Common Sense," *Hindu*, 26 January 1963.

31. One politician said of fourteen-carat gold, "Its colour is ever changing. Gold cannot be a political leader, changing colour every time." S. M. Banerjee in *Lok Sabha Debates*, 3d series, vol. 32, 4 June 1964.

32. J. H. Hutton, *Caste in India*, 3d edition (London: Oxford University Press, 1961). See also Jasleen Dhamija, "Some Aspects of Folk Jewellery," *Marg*, September 1964.

Indians and Pakistanis who twenty years ago fled Partition's havoc
with only what they could carry know the value of gold. Banking
and cooperative society facilities for savings are growing in India,
but they are thinly spread over the Indian countryside and their use
is foreign to many Indians. "The bank and post office may be
closed," the money lenders of Indore told a joint committee of Parliament, "but [an Indian's] own creditor is never closed to him with
his gold securities." [33]

Finally, gold is the citizen's hedge against inflation in an economy
in which the value of money has been steadily depreciating and the
value of gold constantly rising. According to the economist B. R.
Shenoy, "a rustic farmer" who in 1939 invested Rs. 100 in gold
could in 1962 have sold his investment for Rs. 401. The same sum
invested in postal small savings would have appreciated to somewhat under Rs. 300.[34]

In 1958 the Reserve Bank of India estimated the value of the gold
in private hoards in India at Rs. 17.5 billion, at its international
price, and at Rs. 30.35 billion, at its domestic price [35] — a sum almost equal to the total investment in the public sector (Rs. 35.50)
during the Second Five Year Plan, 1956–57 to 1960–61! The Reserve
Bank's distinction between the international and domestic price of
gold must be explained. Gold in India generally sells for more than
twice its price in international markets. This is primarily a result of
short supply and heavy demand in a smugglers' market.[36] India is
only a marginal producer of gold, and since 1947 the government
has prohibited its legal importation. The major suppliers of gold in
India are smugglers, and India has developed into one of the
world's major markets for smuggled gold.

So regular and profitable is the illegal gold trade into India that,
according to B. R. Shenoy, the smugglers have an insurance scheme

33. *Memorandum from the Gold, Silver, and Jawahrat Merchants Association
of Indore* (mimeographed, n.d.).
34. "Basic Factors of the Gold Problem," *Times of India*, 12 November
1964.
35. "Estimates of Gold and Silver Stocks in India," *Reserve Bank of India
Bulletin*, vol. 12, April 1958.
36. At the time the Gold Control Rules were promulgated the international
price for ten grams of gold of a fineness of 0.995, "pure gold," was Rs.
53.58. The prevailing price in India was about Rs. 104, and two and a half
years later it was up to a high of about Rs. 135. The price of gold sold in
"private trading" is quoted regularly in major Indian newspapers.

under which for a 10 to 15 percent premium they can collect the
value of an illegal shipment within twenty-four hours of its
confiscation.[37] It was estimated by the first chief administrator of
the Gold Control Rules that Indians, through a variety of ways of
illegally spending rupees and other currencies abroad and conceal-
ing income earned from foreign trade, purchase about Rs. 400–500
million worth of smuggled gold annually.[38]

For India's economic planners their countrymen's apparently insati-
able appetite for gold was a long, sad story. But there was the possibility of a happy ending. If only domestic savings and earnings
from foreign exchange which were being used to purchase gold
could be made available for investment in modernization!

During the first decade of India's independence, the government
attacked the gold problem through a number of schemes aimed at
curtailing the supply of smuggled gold. These were all unsuccessful.
Spurred on by undiminished demand, the smugglers found ways to
carry on their trade and the illegal flow of gold into India continued. In 1962, the government began to attack its gold problem from
the demand side, and gold prices temporarily sagged. New restrictions were placed on gold trading and new punitive measures were
adopted. The most novel and controversial measure was the first
gold bonds scheme. Bonds were issued that were purchasable for
gold. The purchaser was asked no embarrassing questions about
where the gold came from, and his investment paid a handsome
dividend and was favorably taxed. But the gold was valued at the
international price, and the scheme failed.[39] The Gold Control
Rules of 1963 were a far more direct and massive attack on demand.

After having been approved by the Union Cabinet, the Gold Control Rules were announced by Finance Minister Desai in a radio
broadcast on 9 January 1963.[40] The announcement came without
warning. The government had not consulted with representatives of

37. "Basic Factors."
38. *Free Press Journal*, 17 January 1963. See also, D. K. Rangnekar, *Poverty
and Capital Development in India* (London: Oxford University Press, 1959),
pp. 219–25.
39. According to the Finance Ministry, to January 1963 the scheme had
brought forth from India's hoard only about Rs. 10.9 million. B. R. Bhagat in
Lok Sabha Debates, 3d series, vol. 12, 24 January 1963.
40. *Statesman*, 10 January 1963.

either of the two major and sometimes mutually contentious groups in the gold trade, goldsmiths and jewelers. Nor had it sought the counsel of Congress members of Parliament or leaders of state Congress parties.

The rules were promulgated as an emergency measure. In reaction to the outbreak of Sino-Indian hostilities in 1962, Parliament had granted to the government certain emergency powers for the regulation of war-related domestic affairs. In pursuance of this grant the government had framed the Defence of India Rules, and the Gold Control Rules were amendments to them.[41] According to Morarji Desai, the prime minister had long felt the desirability of a gold control policy.[42] India's conflict with China and, in 1965, its war with Pakistan provided the government with the reason of defense to justify the mobilization of India's gold hoard, an instrument to do the job by extraordinary means, and a seemingly appropriate climate of patriotism.

The crucial and most controversial provision of the rules was "quality control," the prohibition against the manufacture and sale of gold ornaments of a purity greater than fourteen carats. Under this "fourteen-carat rule" smiths were to stop production of high purity gold jewelry immediately and jewelers were given thirty days to clear their stocks of such ornaments. And then no more.

"A newer generation of ornament wearers . . . quietly stringing fountain pen nibs . . . into a garland with fiber glass or nylon" would, according to one irreverent prophet, proclaim "that the Era of the Goldsmiths is gone forever."[43]

The rules, in addition, obliged owners of gold to declare their nonornament holdings above certain nominal limits. They were forbidden to pawn bullion unless it was so declared or to purchase additional bullion. Larger dealers and gold refiners were required to take out licenses in order to carry on their businesses and to maintain records and accounts which might be summoned for inspection, and restrictions were placed on their rights to own and sell gold. A Gold Control Board was established under the chairmanship of G. B. Kotak, a Bombay industrialist and former finance minister of

41. Government of India, Ministry of Law, *Defence of India Act, 1962,* and *Rules under the Defence of India Act, 1962,* 2d ed. (1965).
42. Interview, New Delhi, 30 November 1966.
43. S. Narayanaswamy, "Gold and Common Sense."

Saurashtra, to implement the rules and "to discourage the use and consumption of gold." [44]

In the course of the years to follow, as the rules, amended and re-amended, failed to achieve the results expected of them, the proponents of gold control cut their expectations to fit the rules' achievements. Initially, however, their expectations, or at least their hopes, were great, for nothing less than an "economic revolution," which G. B. Kotak predicted would occur "if the people instead of buying gold invested their money in industrial development." [45]

The revolution's "scenario" was predicated upon the assumption that "quality control" would significantly reduce the demand for gold. It would do so by prohibiting the manufacture and sale of gold ornaments which exceeded the uncustomary and unpopular fineness of fourteen carats. Morarji Desai was adamant in his opposition to any modification of the "fourteen-carat rule": "The old custom of manufacturing ornaments in pure gold had to be abandoned as it retarded the progress of the country." [46] G. B. Kotak said of the rule that "no relaxation . . . could be considered." [47] No compromise, for example, permitting the manufacture of eighteen- or nineteen-carat ornaments was acceptable to the ministry.[48] The object of "quality control" was to debase, to turn gold into tinsel, and by debasing to reduce demand.

In the gold control scenario a reduction in the demand for gold would be followed by a drop in its domestic price, and a drop in its domestic price would lessen the profitability and thus the incidence of smuggling. The illegal flow of rupees out of India to pay for smuggled gold would be dammed and the value of the rupee would appreciate in international money markets.

Indians, responding to the falling value of gold, would less and less convert their surpluses into it, and more and more deposit them in small savings or invest them. Gold itself would be coaxed by its falling value into gold bond schemes. The government's vise on gold production and consumption would be gradually tightened.

44. *Rules*, p. 124.
45. *Hindustan Times*, 7 February 1963.
46. Ibid., 2 February 1963.
47. Ibid., 29 January 1963.
48. An early request made by spokesmen for the gold trade, *Express*, 15 January 1963, and *Hindu*, 22 January 1963.

Further restrictions would be placed on the gold trade, such as for-
bidding dealers to lend money and sell jewelry from the same
premises, and the power of officials to enforce these restrictions
would be increased.[49] The rules' requirement that consumers declare their holdings in gold bullion would be followed by a requirement that they declare their holdings in gold ornaments.[50]

The stick of fear that the government would eventually force gold
holders to sell their treasures to it at the international price, and the
carrot of new and more attractive gold bonds schemes, would drive
more and more gold into the government's coffers. In August 1965
Parliament reluctantly approved a new scheme which offered the
purchasers of bonds bought with "pure gold" repayment after fifteen years in gold of the same fineness, plus dividends, tax concessions, and no questions. Eventually *all* the gold in India would be
in the government's hands. That was the rules' "final objective." [51]

In sum, the rules, in Morarji Desai's words, were conceived to be
a "revolutionary reform," [52] a social as well as an economic reform
which would convert traditional preferences and habits into modern
ones and by so doing carry the converted a few steps further on the
road from tradition to modernity. A new slogan was coined for the
revolution. Indians were to be "weaned away from the lure of
gold." But they would not be weaned, and the smugglers continued
to supply the lure at premium prices. The weaners in the Ministry
of Finance were confronted by widespread noncompliance with
their rules and sympathy for those whom the rules had displaced.
They were unsupported in their efforts by Congress-Government
elites, provincial Congress leaders, and rank-and-file Congress politicians, and were actively opposed by opposition politicians and
new organizations in the gold trade. Apparently in response to this
general and mounting disapproval, Morarji Desai's successor, T. T.
Krishnamachari, announced in September 1963 a "concession" on
the "fourteen-carat rule" to self-employed goldsmiths. But the effects
of this "concession" were to mobilize opposition among jewelers

49. The rules were so amended in June 1963.
50. The Gold (Control) Act which was passed by Parliament in December
1964 provided for such declarations. Amendments to the rules which became
effective in November 1966 also called for the declaration of ornament holdings.
51. Speech by Morarji Desai in the Rajya Sabha, *Hindu,* 15 March 1963.
52. *Express,* 25 March 1963.

without demobilizing it among goldsmiths, and to reduce even further the government's already minimal capacity to enforce its policy. Three years later the government, in spite of "expert" advice to the contrary, abandoned "quality control" altogether and with it any expectation that the gold control scenario would ever be played.

3   INTEREST GROUPS

This chapter is concerned primarily with the structure of nonparty interest groups and their interrelationships. There are at least two obvious and important structural differences between the groups in the two cases. First, the groups which opposed the Congress-Government elite's states reorganization policies in western India were regional groups with large, concentrated constituencies. The groups that opposed the Gold Control Rules were nationwide with relatively small, scattered constituencies. The effects of this difference on the oppositional processes in the two cases will be treated in this and succeeding chapters.

Second, the interest groups which opposed the rules were founded and maintained as trade associations autonomous of the political party system. The nonparty groups which supported the linguistic-provincial movements in western India were organized into associations, particularly in Maharashtra, by political parties or coalitions of political parties. But no linguistic-provincial movement in western India was totally encapsulated by a particular party, or coalition of political parties, or linguistic-provincial association. Thus, for example, the movement for Samyukta Maharashtra was supported by representatives of all the nonparty groups in Maharashtra — in this study, castes. But representatives of the same groups were associated with either the Maharashtra Congress or the anti-Congress-Government Samyukta Maharashtra Samiti. In other words, the same movement was organizationally sustained by and divided between rival political associations. This same division was present to a lesser extent among the generally contentious party components of the samiti. The peasant proprietors, businessmen, students, weavers, Brahman lawyers, and so forth who made up the other linguistic-provincial movements in western India were affiliated with and divided among political organizations, but these

29

movements were generally less dependent on political organizations for their associational forms than the movement in Maharashtra.

In sum, linguistic-provincialism in western India had two interrelated and overlapping personalities between which it is possible, for the sake of analysis, to make a somewhat arbitrary distinction: movements composed of nonparty groups and associations composed of parties. This chapter will deal with the former, and chapters 4 and 5 with the latter. Associations in the gold trade will also be dealt with here.

Beyond these differences, structural and interrelational characteristics of the groups in both cases are strikingly similar. In both cases groups were formed in response to Congress-Government policies or impending policies, or in response to the formation of other groups. Linguistic-provincial associations and national associations in the gold trade developed from already existing secondary associations and nonassociational groups. The formation of these new associations affected, at least temporarily, the alignments within and among preexisting groups. Organization in both cases radiated from urban centers and urban leaders. Both cases were resolved when the government yielded to minimal group demands. The associations and the movements then disintegrated or lapsed into quietude.

Maharashtra, Mahavidarbha, and Mahagujarat

Although the movement for Samyukta Maharashtra was not the first linguistic-provincial movement in western India, it was without doubt the most widely and intensely supported, and thus the most threatening to Congress's "dominant" position in the area. It was Maharashtrian linguistic-provincialism which pressed most heavily on the national Congress-Government elite and activated the renegotiations which eventually culminated in the Bombay Reorganization Act of 1960. Opponents of Samyukta Maharashtra in Gujarat, Nag-Vidarbha, and Bombay city, after initially coming to favorable terms with the Congress-Government elite, were compelled to come to terms with the Marhattas.

Nowhere in western India did the multilingual status quo of 1955 or the alternatives to it proposed by the States Reorganization

Commission and the Congress Working Committee engender such dissatisfaction as they did in Maharashtra. This was clear no later than February 1957. Although Congress won the second general elections in bilingual Bombay, it suffered a massive defeat in Maharashtra. And insofar as dissatisfaction can be measured by indexes such as public disorder and defections from Congress, it was clear long before the elections.

When the Samyukta Maharashtra Parishad was formed in 1946, Congress's commitment to linguistic-provincialism was still intact. The parishad, therefore, was not founded to oppose anything, but rather to stake out the territorial claims of Marhattas in anticipation of the post-Independence linguistic-provincial reorganization of India. Over the next decade and a half, however, after having its ambitions frustrated by the Dar Commission, the JVP Committee, the States Reorganization Commission, the Congress Working Committee, and the Government of India, the parishad and the movement it represented developed and deepened into an oppositional front against what its spokesmen more and more characterized as the anti-Maharashtrianism of the Congress's "presiding deities." [1] For example, the president of the Maharashtra PCC accused the States Reorganization Commission of being "prejudiced and biased against Maharashtrians" and compared its recommendation for keeping Marathi-speakers divided between Bombay and Nag-Vidarbha to the "partitioning of Bengal by Lord Curzon in the olden days." [2]

Linguistic-provincialism in Maharashtra was fired emotionally by memories of past glory and reminders of present distress. The Marhattas were, after all, the people of Shivaji Maharaj who in the seventeenth century humbled the Moguls and ruled the western Deccan! Now the Marhattas, who had "a tradition among traditionless people," were being humbled and denied a state of their own. They and only they. And by whom? The Gujarati "capitalists" of Bombay city, "the upstart people of yesterday who came . . . for profit, in the wake of foreign traders and foreign government," [3] and

1. N. G. Goray, *Express*, 19 February 1959.

2. T. R. Deogirikar, *Twelve Years in Parliament: Democracy in Action* (Poona: Chitrashala Prakashan, 1964), p. 194.

3. G. V. Deshmukh, *Maharashtra Unification Conference*, Bombay, 16 October 1948.

established their colony in the Maharashtrian city of Bombay, in which Maharashtrians now labored as "clerks and coolies." [4]

The movement did not lose its fervor when the Maharashtra PCC withdrew from the parishad in January 1956. It merely fragmented into three associations: the Maharashtra PCC; the Samyukta Maharashtra Samiti, a coalition of almost all the opposition parties in Maharashtra; and somewhere between them the Samyukta Maharashtra Congress Jana Parishad, an organization of dissident Congressmen from Bombay city affiliated with the samiti. The associations were politically competitive, but their goal was the same: the creation of Samyukta Maharashtra with its capital at Bombay city. If anything, the movement's dedication to this goal was reinforced as the associations vied with each other.

In no small measure, the persistence of the movement for Samyukta Maharashtra was a result of its widespread support among members of the three major caste groups of Maharashtra: Marathas, scheduled castes, and Brahmans.[5] Its support by Brahmans and scheduled castes requires some explanation, since it was generally recognized and accepted that Samyukta Maharashtra would be "Maratha Raj." That is, the general expectation was that political life in a Marhatta state would be dominated by the state's "dominant caste," the Marathas. In Samyukta Maharashtra, every third person would be a Maratha. In contrast, the Marathas were about 15 percent of the population in "big bilingual" Bombay, and in "balanced bilingual" Bombay they would have been about 13 percent.[6] For the scheduled castes the Marathas are traditional taskmasters, and for the Brahmans they are the leaders of one of modern India's oldest anti-Brahman movements.

Although they are few in number, only about 4 percent of the population of Maharashtra, the Brahmans have traditionally domi-

4. B. R. Ambedkar, *Thoughts on Linguistic States* (1955). It might be added that at one point S. M. Joshi, the principal Praja Socialist leader of the Samyukta Maharashtra movement, caused a stir of sufficient magnitude to involve the prime minister by accusing Morarji Desai, the first among Gujarati Congressmen, of having slandered Shivaji in an interview with an American student; *Express*, 1 November 1957.

5. These are really agglomerations of caste units rather than castes. But we are dealing with political units in a particular case, and the term "caste group" is sufficiently accurate for our purposes.

6. Basic figures from the *Census of India, 1931*, reprinted in Samyukta Maharashtra Parishad, *United Maharashtra* (Bombay, 1948).

nated the intellectual, social, and political life of the area. The Sa-tyashodhak Samaj was founded in 1873 by Jyotiba Phule, a leader of the Mali caste, partly to reduce that dominance. It was reduced, although certainly not eliminated, in the Maharashtra PCC. But non-Brahman politicians have been less successful in replacing Brahman leadership in the national opposition parties in Maharash-tra and have instead formed a few parties whose leadership is non-Brahman and whose operations are limited to Maharashtra.

Since the 1920s the Satyashodhak Samaj and the anti-Brahman movement, in general, have been in the hands of Marathas. In the twenties the Samaj "conducted various activities" in parts of Maha-rashtra which were "designed to harass Brahmans," [7] and in 1948 there were anti-Brahman disturbances in various parts of Maharash-tra following Gandhi's assassination by a Maharashtrian Brahman.

The most prominant Satyashodhak leader of the recent past was Keshavrao Jedhe. Jedhe was a Maratha. He lead the Marathas into Congress in the thirties; after Gandhi's assassination he left Con-gress to found a Maratha political party, the Shetkari Kamkari Paksh, and he returned to Congress in 1954. He was also one of the five vice-presidents of the Samyukta Maharashtra Parishad. But the president was a Brahman.

As a group, Brahmans neither supported nor opposed Samyukta Maharashtra. However, a vastly disproportionate number of the movement's leaders were Brahmans. To mention only the most prominent: Mahamahopadhyaya D. V. Potdar, one of the founders of the parishad; Shankarrao Deo, the president of the parishad; Pro-fessor D. R. Gadgil, the parishad's major theoretician and publicist; N. V. Gadgil, the most uncompromising supporter of the movement within the Congress, S. A. Dange, Communist leader and president of the Samyukta Maharashtra Samiti; S. M. Joshi, Praja Socialist leader and general secretary of the samiti; and P. K. Atre, author, publisher, and the samiti's chief whip in the Bombay Legislative As-sembly.

This situation was not without its ironies. D. R. Gadgil reported that, at least initially, some Marathas stayed away from the paris-had because they thought it was a Brahman organization.[8] The samiti, although more uncompromising in its demand for Samyukta

7. Maureen L. P. Patterson, "Caste and Political Leadership in Maharash-tra," *Economic Weekly*, 25 September 1954.
8. Interview, Poona, 25 April 1967.

Maharashtra than the Maharashtra PCC, was handicapped, according to S. M. Joshi, because most of the samiti's leaders were Brahmans, whereas most of the leading Maratha politicians — Jedhe,
Yashwantrao Chavan, and Bhausaheb Hiray — were Congressmen.[9]

It is tempting to imagine that the Maharashtrian Brahmans acted
with enlightened self-interest, the upper-dog's grace; that, confronted by the inevitable, they chose to lead it. There was some of
this, but it was not very significant politically. Brahman associations
played a relatively minor role in the movement for Samyukta Maharashtra. The Hindu Sabha and the Jana Sangh, perhaps the most
Brahman-oriented parties in Maharashtra, were minor members of
the Samyukta Maharashtra Samiti. The sanghis entered the samiti
reluctantly and withdrew early, more out of fear of a "leftist consolidation" in the samiti than of "Maratha Raj," which they along with
everyone else accepted as inevitable.[10] Neither the sangh nor the
sabha provided the Samyukta Maharashtra movement with any of
its principal leaders.

For the most part, the Brahman leaders of the movement were
what N. G. Goray, one of them, called "declassed elements." [11] Perhaps they should more accurately be called "decasted elements."
This is not to say that they were unaware of or indifferent to caste.
Few Indian politicians can afford that luxury. But the Brahman
politicians in Maharashtra were not caste politicians. Their constituencies were not their castes, and their interests were not caste interests. Among some, awareness of caste manifested itself in a certain noblesse oblige, the aristocrat's willingness to preside over his
succession, not unmixed, to be sure, with condescension for successors who "can hardly write their names." [12] Who but Brahmans
could lead the movement, asked one who had led it, when the Marathas are "intellectually inferior?" [13]

Some Brahman politicians had reservations. But as politicians
they cast them aside without much difficulty. For example, T. R.
Deogirikar said that he did not associate himself with the Samyukta
Maharashtra Parishad because he felt, among other things, that "in

9. Interview, New Delhi, 4 April 1967.
10. *Bombay Chronicle,* 20 January 1958.
11. Interview, Poona, 24 April 1967.
12. A comment on the *nouveau régime* from one of its Brahman founders,
Poona, 24 April 1967.
13. Interview, Bombay, 22 April 1967.

a multilingual state Brahmans have some chance." [14] But Deogirikar
was the president of the Maharashtra PCC between 1955 and 1958,
and as such actively supported Samyukta Maharashtra. Opposition
leaders like S. A. Dange and S. M. Joshi are best understood as
leftist and anti-Congress rather than Brahman politicians.

Finally, if any Brahmans had thought that their positions of leadership in the Samyukta Maharashtra movement would turn into positions of power in Maharashtra state, they miscalculated. To be
sure, their efforts have not gone unrecognized. The vice-chancellor-
ship of the University of Poona, for example, was held continuously
between 1962 and 1967 by distinguished Brahman scholars who
supported the movement.[15] Although they were routed at the polls
in 1962, Brahmans continued to lead the opposition.[16] But the politics of Maharashtra have been dominated by Congress since the
state's inception, and Brahman influence in Congress has, if anything, continued to decline. Some Brahmans who were active in the
movement now complain of extralegal discriminations against Brahmans by the state government.

At one point in 1960, S. M. Joshi declared that one of the major
achievements of the Samyukta Maharashtra movement was to bring
the three major caste groups in Maharashtra together in a common
effort, to create a "new synthesis." The "synthesis" was short lived.
V. M. Sirsikar concludes his study of voting behavior in the 1962
general elections in Poona, one of the strongholds of the movement,
as follows:

> The role of caste was to a certain extent over-shadowed by the emo-
> tionally charged atmosphere of the 1957 elections in Maharashtra. But
> this could not be considered as a permanent phenomenon. The 1962 elec-
> tions to a certain extent have indicated the transient character of non-
> caste voting behavior witnessed earlier.[17]

In sharp contrast to the Brahmans, the scheduled castes, at the
bottom of the caste ladder, are explicitly organized for political action. The Scheduled Castes Federation was founded in 1942, and

14. Interview, Poona, 24 April 1967.
15. D. V. Potdar, N. V. Gadgil, and D. R. Gadgil.
16. S. A. Dange, N. G. Goray, and P. K. Atre were defeated for the Lok
Sabha, and S. M. Joshi was defeated for the legislative assembly. P. K. Atre won
a legislative assembly seat. Election Commission, *Report on the Third General
Elections in India, 1962*, 2 (Statistical): 41, 264.
17. V. M. Sirsikar, *Political Behaviour in India* (Bombay: Manaktalas,
1965), p. 247.

changed its name to the Republican Party of India (RPI) in 1957. The backbone of the RPI is Maharashtra's most numerous and ubiquitous scheduled caste, the Mahars. Between 1956 and 1957 about 50 percent of Maharashtra's scheduled caste members, most of them Mahars, converted to Buddhism in an effort to escape from the degraded position assigned to them by Hindus.[18] The total scheduled caste (including Neo-Buddhist) population of Maharashtra is about 13 percent.

Until he died in 1956, the leading spokesman for the scheduled castes was Dr. B. R. Ambedkar. Ambedkar was a Mahar, the founder of the Scheduled Castes Federation, and the leader of scheduled castes in their conversion to Buddhism. In 1948 it was Ambedkar's position that "all parts of Maharashtra should be merged together in a single province," and that the Akola Pact represented only "the wish of a few high caste politicians who feel that in a unified Maharashtra their political careers will come to an end." [19] But by 1955 he had concluded that "in our country linguism is another name for communalism. When you create a linguistic province you hand over the strings of administration to . . . the majority community." [20] Instead of a single Maharashtra state he proposed that there be four. Bombay city would be renamed "Maharashtra City State." "Western Maharashtra," with a scheduled caste population of about 9 percent, would be formed from the Marathi-speaking districts of Bombay state minus some southeastern districts with heavy scheduled caste populations. These coupled with Marathwada would form "Central Maharashtra," whose scheduled caste population would be about 14 percent. "Eastern Maharashtra," with a scheduled caste population of about 18 percent, would be formed from Nag-Vidarbha. It might be noted that Ambedkar received a Ph.D. in economics from Columbia University in 1917. He was knowledgeable about American politics, and presumably this knowledgeability extended to the institution of the gerrymandered district.

18. For a discussion of this and other aspects of scheduled caste politics in Maharashtra see Eleanor Zelliot, "Buddhism and Politics in Maharashtra," in *South Asian Politics and Religion*, edited by Donald Eugene Smith (Princeton, N.J.: Princeton University Press, 1966).

19. B. R. Ambedkar, *Maharashtra as a Linguistic Province: A Statement Submitted to the Linguistic Provinces Commission* (Bombay: Thacker and Co., 1948).

20. Quoted in Deogirikar, *Twelve Years in Parliament*, p. 147.

From Ambedkar's point of view this "four-unit" scheme had several advantages. It preserved language as the basis for states reorganization, a position he had committed himself to earlier, and it divided a large and heavily populated territory into more administratively manageable areas. But primarily it held out the promise of giving the scheduled castes more protection and more political influence. "Maharashtra City State," in which the Marathas would not be an influential minority, would provide an asylum for untouchables who wished to flee from tyranny and oppression in the villages. Four state governments would provide more opportunities and more influence for scheduled castes than one, particularly in "Central" and "Eastern Maharashtra," where they would account for a higher percentage of the population than they would in a unified Maharashtra. In Ambedkar's words: "The larger the state the smaller the proportion of the minority to the majority. . . . A small stone of a consolidated majority placed on the chest of the minority may be borne. But the weight of a huge mountain it cannot bear." [21] Or less metaphorically and more to the point, in the words of S. L. Kamble, one of Ambedkar's heirs, it was "with the object of securing the due interests of the Scheduled Castes and other minorities that the late Dr. Babasaheb Ambedkar suggested the creation of small standard states and the division of Maharashtra into four states." [22]

Whatever the merits of Ambedkar's scheme may have been, the political power of the RPI in Maharashtra was never great enough to compel the Congress or the Samyukta Maharashtra Samiti to consider it as a real alternative. Perhaps Ambedkar realized this, for he did not actively campaign either for or against Samyukta Maharashtra. For the Republicans in Maharashtra, the real alternatives were either joining the samiti coalition and getting what they could from it or going it alone and perhaps suffering the same fate as had the Socialists (a group separate from the Praja Socialists), who did not join the samiti and were literally wiped off the political map of Maharashtra in the 1957 general elections. They joined.

The interests and sympathies engaged in the Samyukta Maharashtra movement and the countermovements it engendered in Nag-Vi-

21. Ambedkar, *Thoughts on Linguistic States*.
22. Bombay, *Legislative Assembly Debates*, vol. 10, part 2, 16 March 1960.

darbha, Bombay city, and Gujarat were many and diverse: economic, linguistic, ideological, caste, and political. Some interests
and sympathies overlapped and reinforced each other. Complementary interests brought otherwise separate groups together, as they
did in Maharashtra, and diverging interests and differing situations
fragmented other groups. But the movements all radiated from cities. A capital city was the prize sought or defended most ardently
by all movements, and the most ardent supporters of every movement were from these cities.

The headquarters of the Samyukta Maharashtra movement were
in Bombay city and Poona, the headquarters of its leaders, its linguistic-provincial associations and political parties, and their supporting structures, such as the University of Poona, literary societies, newspapers, and the Municipal Corporation and non-Congress
labor unions of Bombay city.

Bombay city was the cockpit in which Maharashtrian "clerks and
coolies" and Gujarati "capitalists" stood face-to-face. The nature of
the relationship between them in Bombay city (and to a lesser extent in Nagpur city) helped to mobilize a "left front" in favor of Samyukta Maharashtra and gave the movement its anticapitalist élan.
The largest group of Congress dissidents were from Bombay city. The
largest group of dissenting-but-disciplined Congressmen, those who
refused to be reconciled to the "three-unit" solution, were from
the city's neighboring district of Ratnagiri, which supplies the city
with a number of migrant workers almost equal to the total number
of migrants from all other parts of Maharashtra.[23] The movement
for Samyukta Maharashtra was most active, militant, and violent in
Bombay city. Bombay city was its first prize, and was the rock in
western India on which linguistic-provincial reorganization foun-
dered.

The "movement" to retain Gujarati control over Bombay city was
supported most strenuously by Gujaratis in the city, and by those
with commercial and financial ties to it and them. By the late 1950s
the Mahavidarbha movement had shrunk to the confines of Nagpur
city. Outside Ahmadabad city, the movement for Mahagujarat was
largely restricted to the neighboring districts of Ahmadabad, Kaira,

23. *Census of India*, 1961, vol. 10, Maharashtra, part 10 (1-C), Greater
Bombay Special Migration Tables, 1966, p. 62.

and Mehsana, which supply the city with half its immigrant population.[24]

To the leaders of the Samyukta Maharashtra movement, the Marathwada area of Hyderabad and Nag-Vidarbha in Madhya Pradesh were Maharashtra irredenta.

> Barring the accident of administrative history from the eighteenth to the twentieth century there is nothing that logically separates Nagpur-Berar [Nag-Vidarbha], Marathwada, [and] west Maharashtra. . . . In neither the physical, geographical, historical, cultural, linguistic, or social conditions are there any factors which markedly distinguish one area in the territory of Maharashtra from another in such a manner as to justify the formation of a separate political unit.[25]

In Marathwada there was no countermovement of any significance. The Mahavidarbha movement, which began among Congressmen in Berar and had been largely ignored in the renegotiations which followed the States Reorganization Commission's report, resurfaced in bilingual Bombay as opposition to be reconciled. Its center, however, had shifted eastward to Nagpur city, and it was largely confined there.

A seminar on the "Problems of Maharashtra" held in 1959 under the auspices of the Indian Committee for Cultural Freedom concluded that "the experience of [Nag-] Vidarbha during the last few years of its integration with Bombay has not been very happy." [26] Two years earlier a new organization based in Nagpur city, the Nag-Vidarbha Andolan Samiti (the Nag-Vidarbha Agitation Committee), had been founded to press for the creation of Mahavidarbha. The Andolan Samiti was outside Congress, although it was supported by Congressmen, among others. The most effective support for Mahavidarbha, however, came from the Nagpur Congress organization itself. Congress was the only political organization of any consequence in Nagpur, and by 1959 its position was clear: if bilingual Bombay was going to be divided it should be into three parts, Maharashtra, Gujarat, *and Mahavidarbha.*

24. Ibid., vol. 5, Gujarat, part X-C, Special Migrant Tables, Ahmadabad City, 1966.

25. Samyukta Maharashtra Parishad, *Reorganization of States in India with Particular Reference to the Formation of Maharashtra* (Bombay, 1954).

26. Indian Committee for Cultural Freedom, *Problems of Maharashtra* (Bombay, 1960), p. 136.

Less than a month after the Congress-Government elite had decided to reopen the issue of reorganization, the municipal corporation of Nagpur city,[27] the Mahavidarbha Chamber of Commerce in Nagpur city,[28] the Nagpur Regional Congress Committee [29] and the Nagpur branch of the Congress-dominated Indian National Trade Union Congress (INTUC) [30] resolved themselves in favor of the creation of Mahavidarbha.

In Vidarbha, on the other hand, the movement for Mahavidarbha had dissipated over the years. Gopalrao Khedkar, the president of the Vidarbha PCC, had signed the Nagpur Pact and was an active advocate of Samyukta Maharashtra. And with the impending division of Bombay state, the majority of Vidarbha's delegation to Parliament [31] and the Vidarbha RCC [32] declared themselves in favor of joining Samyukta Maharashtra.

Although the Marathi-speaking caste populations of the Nagpur and Vidarbha districts are similar, the Vidarbha Congress was far more heavily under the influence of Marathas than the Nagpur Congress. This difference is crucial in explaining the different preferences of the two groups. But the answers to why this difference existed, and how in Nagpur it resulted in the perpetuation of the Mahavidarbha movement, lie in Nagpur city.

The Mahavidarbha movement in the late fifties was united by the fear of "Maratha Raj," in general. But in particular, its unifying apprehension was that Nagpur city, which had been a capital city of the Bhonsla Rajas, the British Central Provinces, and Madhya Pradesh in the Indian Union, would be overshadowed and exploited in Samyukta Maharashtra by Bombay city and Poona. In Samyukta Maharashtra, Nagpur would become merely another provincial town. It would deteriorate and the interests of groups in and around it would be neglected. Who were these groups? Non-Marathi-speaking businessmen from Gujarat, Rajasthan (Marwaris), and Mahakoshal (the Hindi-speaking area of Madhya Pradesh); the Koshtis, a caste of weavers in Nagpur city; local scheduled castes; and Marathi-speaking Brahmans, many of them lawyers.

27. *Free Press Journal*, 6 September 1959.
28. *Hitavada*, 9 September 1959.
29. In bilingual Bombay the various PCCs were reduced, in name, to Regional Congress Committees (RCCs) under one statewide Bombay PCC.
30. *Amrita Bazar Patrika*, 3 September 1959.
31. *Free Press Journal*, 7 September 1959.
32. *Deccan Herald*, 17 September 1959.

Supporters of Samyukta Maharashtra were quick to dismiss the Mahavidarbha movement as one "dominated by non-Marathi vested interests." [33] The Marhattas, by and large, have not been a mercantile people, and much of their commerce, not only in Bombay city but throughout Maharashtra, is in the hands of non-Marhattas, particularly Gujaratis. In the cities in which they congregate and dominate commerce and industry, non-Marathi-speaking businessmen have turned to Congress and government, and to the domination of Congress and government, to protect their interests. This has been the case in Bombay and Nagpur cities.

The businessmen of Nagpur wanted their city to remain a state capital. For them the relocation of legislators, government servants and offices, and all that would follow in their train to Bombay city were translatable into losses in rents, sales, customers, land values, and contracts. But these immediate losses were not all they feared. The businessmen of Nagpur city were apprehensive that a state government in Bombay city — the source from which licenses, permits, contracts, and favors would then flow — would not only be spatially distant — an inconvenience and an expense in itself — but would be politically distant — "wooden" and lacking the "personal touch" of the government they knew in Nagpur city.[34] The government in Bombay city might be of Marathas or Marhattas, but it would not be theirs.

Neither the Koshtis nor the scheduled castes of Nagpur fall into the category of "non-Marathi vested interests." They are poor people who speak Marathi, but both had interests in retaining their state capital at Nagpur city. The Koshtis are cottage industry, handloom weavers. Their fear was that without the protection of "their" government, they would fall victims to the power looms of Bombay city.[35] The scheduled castes of Nagpur under the leadership of Haridas Awade broke with the RPI leadership in Bombay to support Mahavidarbha, Ambedkar's "Eastern Maharashtra."

One of the founders of the Andolan Samiti was T. G. Deshmukh, a Brahman and a lawyer in Nagpur city. Deshmukh's associate, Dr. M. S. Aney, also a Brahman and a lawyer, was the Mahavidarbha

33. For example, *A Supplementary Memorandum Submitted by the Nag-Vidarbha Samiti of the Samyukta Maharashtra Parishad to the States Reorganization Commission* (1954), p. 15.

34. Interviews, New Delhi, Nagpur, and Bhopal.

35. Narendra Deoghare, M.P., interview, New Delhi, 20 April 1967.

movement's "veteran and undisputed leader." [36] The clearest exposition of the Brahmans' case against Samyukta Maharashtra was made by Aney. It was a case compounded of opposition to reducing Nagpur city to a "second-rate or third-rate town," to the cultural imperialism of western Maharashtrian Brahmans, and to "Maratha Raj." [37]

A substantial number of Nagpur's lawyers are Brahmans. Lawyers' interests in keeping a state capital and particularly its high court are self-evident. The signers of the Nagpur Pact had attempted to reconcile them to Samyukta Maharashtra by promising a second seat of the state's high court at Nagpur city, "adequate representation in respect of appointments from the services and the bar," and "at least one" session of the state legislative assembly each year in Nagpur city.[38] But the Nagpur Pact had been "tossed into the dustbin" [39] with the creation of bilingual Bombay, and there was no assurance that it would ever be retrieved.

Scholars in Nag-Vidarbha, traditionally Brahmans, according to Aney had developed an "inferiority complex" because the patterns for Marathi language and literature since the nineteenth century were being set in Poona and Bombay. Nag-Vidarbha could not develop culturally if it continued "under the overhanging branches" of western Maharashtrian influence.[40] The principal of the Government Law College in Bombay, T. K. Tope, put it this way: "The educated people of Vidarbha have their own misgivings about Poona: so much so that a few of them told me as [far] back as 1952 that they were prepared to come into Maharashtra provided Poona is kept out of it." [41]

Aney's particular ire was directed at the Satyashodhak movement which, he wrote, had spread "communal hatred and sectarian jealousy" in western Maharashtra, and "contaminated and vitiated" the lower classes in Satara and Kolhapur districts. The teachings of Maharashtra's great men, according to Aney, had "not yet penetrated deep enough to break the barriers of communalism and the spirit of

---

36. *Hitavada,* 30 August 1959.

37. Madhao Shrihari Aney, *Memorandum Submitted to the States Reorganization Commission* (Yeotmal: Yeotmal District Association, n.d.).

38. Text reproduced in Samyukta Maharashtra Parishad, *Reorganization of States,* p. 109.

39. *Hitavada,* 10 September 1959.

40. Aney, *Memorandum.*

41. T. K. Tope, "Social Problems of Maharashtra," in *Problems of Maharashtra.*

jealousy and antagonism in a large section of the [Maharashtrian] population which has now the right to vote and rule the country." Therefore, he considered it "wrong to bring any other blocs of large population which are comparatively free from these pernicious traits under their political authority and dominant interest." [42]

Although the Mahavidarbha movement divided Marathi-speaker from Marathi-speaker, scheduled caste from scheduled caste, and Brahman from Brahman across regional lines, it papered over the political split in Nag-Vidarbha between Brahmans and the *bhujan samaj* — everyone else.[43] The Nag-Vidarbha Andolan Samiti, in part, served the function of bringing Brahmans who were largely excluded from leadership positions in the Nagpur PCC into the Mahavidarbha movement. But even the Nagpur Congress's *bhujan samaj* made some concessions. In 1959 it turned to Aney, as the most renowned champion of Mahavidarbha, to be its candidate in the by-election for the parliamentary seat from Nagpur city. He won. But after the Congress-Government elite's decision to create Samyukta Maharashtra had been made and accepted by the Nagpur PCC, Aney left Congress and associated himself completely with the Andolan Samiti. In the samiti's final days, Aney shared its leadership, inharmoniously, with another prominent Congress defector, Brijlal Biyani. It was hardly the first time the two had met. Biyani, a Marwari, had been instrumental in the 1930s in relieving the Vidarbha PCC of its Brahman leadership, a leadership typified by M. S. Aney, who had been its president from 1921 to 1930. [44]

Because the new state government was successful in relieving the fears of Nag-Vidarbha's Congress politicians and nonparty groups, and because the worst of these fears never materialized, the Mahavidarbha movement did not long survive the incorporation of Nagpur and Vidarbha into Samyukta Maharashtra. Aney, who attended it at its birth, saw it to its pyre. In the 1967 general elections, at the

42. Aney, *Memorandum.*
43. Literally a community of commoners, actually a euphemism for an association from which Brahmans are excluded.
44. Punjabrao Deshmukh, then Union minister for agriculture, a leader of the Vidarbha PCC, a Samyukta Maharashtra advocate, and a former protégé of Biyani, said at one point that his old mentor had no right to speak for Vidarbha since he (Biyani) "belonged" to the Hindi- rather than Marathi-speaking people: *Hitavada*, 16 April 1959. Biyani, who had been Vidarbha PCC president for thirteen years, answered by sharply rebuking Deshmukh for "linguism" and for forgetting that "when one assumes power, one need not forget the right principles and the past happenings." Ibid., 22 April 1959.

age of eighty-seven, he defended his seat in Parliament as an Independent, still committed to Mahavidarbha. His challenger was Narendra Deoghare, a Koshti leader and a Congressman. Deoghare
won, and Aney lost his deposit. But by then, in the words of one of
the founders of the Andolan Samiti, the Mahavidarbha movement
was "of historical interest only." [45]

Bombay city is the milch cow of western India — the second largest
urban concentration in India, a great capital city and business center. It is an employment market not only for local people but for
migrants from all over India, the source of a great deal of India's
industrial and commercial wealth, remittance income for people in
its hinterlands, and revenue for the state over which it presides.

The battle for Bombay city was the crux of the struggle for Samyukta Maharashtra. Although the Congress-Government elite in
1956 was quite willing to brush aside the recommendation of the
States Reorganization Commission and its predecessors for a separate Mahavidarbha and combine Nag-Vidarbha and Maharashtra
into one state, it was adamant until 1959 in its refusal to establish
Bombay city as the capital of Maharashtra. But the Samyukta Maharashtra movement was no less adamant. Its leaders argued that
by all rights the city belonged to Maharashtra. Its original inhabi-
tants spoke Marathi, the largest single linguistic group in the city
were Marathi-speakers, and the largest urban concentration of Marathi-speakers anywhere was in the city. Bombay city was a major
Marhatta cultural center, job market, and source of remittance income. The transportation and communication systems of Maharashtra were oriented to Bombay city, and the city's power and water
and labor were supplied by Maharashtra. In short: "Bombay is a
[Marhatta] city with Maharashtra . . . as its hinterland." [46]

As in Nagpur, the leaders of the Samyukta Maharashtra movement faced their antagonists in Bombay city across the overlapping
barriers of class and language. There was some caste overtone to
the struggle, but not much. The Gujarati, Parsi, Marwari, and Sin-
dhi industrialists and merchants who spoke through the Bombay
PCC, the Bombay Citizens' Committee, the Indian Merchants'
Chamber, and Gujarati associations outside Bombay city might
have been more willing to accept Samyukta Maharashtra had they

45. Sureshchandra Gangrede, interview, Bhopal, 17 April 1967.
46. Samyukta Maharashtra Parishad, *Reorganization of States.*

thought that it would be ruled by worldly and friendly Marhatta Brahmans like S. K. Patil, the president of the Bombay PCC, or B. G. Kher, the late chief minister of Bombay state.[47] But this, of course, was not to be the case.

The case for the non-Marhatta business community in Bombay city was that its control over the city was being challenged not only by a linguistic movement but by a movement which proclaimed itself to be hostile to "capitalism" in general and to their "capitalism" in particular.[48] The Samyukta Maharashtra Samiti was for the most part a coalition of leftist parties in which the Communists played an increasingly dominant role. Its leaders were outspokenly antagonistic to the "capitalist system," and blamed that system both for pauperizing the Marhattas in Bombay city and for denying the city to Samyukta Maharashtra. But it was not only the samiti and the Communists. This "radical socialism" which the city's industrialists feared was not absent from the pronouncements of Maharashtrian Congressmen.[49] The Bombay Citizens' Committee, which had argued against the incorporation of Bombay city into a unilingual Maharashtra before the Dar Commission and was reconstitued to press the same arguments before the States Reorganization Commission, quoted the Maharashtra Congress leader N. V. Gadgil as having said "If Bombay is made the capital of Maharashtra we shall see that the rich as a class are wiped out."[50]

The Citizens' Committee described itself as being constituted of "leading citizens of Bombay representing different sections of the population." The different economic sections were almost exclusively business and the professions. Among the businessmen were almost all the great names in Indian commerce and industry: Tata, Birla, Kilachand, Mody. The different communal sections were, by and large, Gujarati, Parsi, Marwari, and Muslim business communities from Gujarat. A Marhatta section was conspicuous by its ab-

---

47. Both men were opponents of the inclusion of Bombay city in Samyukta Maharashtra. B. G. Kher was quoted by another Brahman, a particularly reliable interviewee, as having said to him, "We don't want Jedhes [Satyashodakh anti-Brahmans] ruling Bombay."

48. It might be noted that the Maharashtra Chamber of Commerce, which was located in Bombay city but was more representative of Marhatta-owned enterprises and enterprises outside Bombay city than the Indian Merchants' Chamber, supported Samyukta Maharashtra.

49. U. N. Dhebar, interview, New Delhi, 12 April 1967.

50. *Memorandum,* Submitted to the States Reorganization Commission (1954).

sence. Of the 101 names of its members listed by the Citizens' Committee no more than three were Marhatta, and none of these were
officers.[51]

A proposal made by D. R. Gadgil and published by the Maharashtra parishad for the "compulsory decentralization" of the city's
industries so that Bombay city would "exist chiefly as the port and
economic center of Maharashtra" was hardly calculated to reassure
the "vested interests." Early in the movement's history, G. V. Deshmukh "put it plainly":

> Are Maharashtrians content . . . [with] playing the part of secondary
> brokers to brokers, secondary agents to agents, assistant professors to pro-
> fessors, clerks to managers [and] hired labourers to shopkeepers.[52]

The fears of the non-Marhatta business community were not only
fears of words and plans. Between 1956 and 1960 politically in-
spired strikes and violence aimed at Gujaratis erupted periodically
in Bombay city. With its large population of disaffected Marhattas
and its large non-Congress labor unions under the direction of the
leftist leaders of the Samyukta Maharashtra Samiti, Bombay city
was the most active and violent center of the Samyukta Maharashtra movement.[53]

Of course, the business community and its allies argued against
making Bombay city the capital of Maharashtra from the "larger
perspective of the national interest." [54] But they also argued from
the perspective of *their* interests, and did so with considerable can-
dor. Bombay city was theirs. It had been made by them, and they
stood to lose from its incorporation into Maharashtra.

51. Ibid.
52. *Maharashtra Unification Conference.*
53. Interviews, New Delhi, Bombay, and Poona. S. A. Dange, for example,
has been both president and general secretary of the Communist-led All India
Trade Union Congress (AITUC). S. M. Joshi is also a leading trade unionist.
54. C. L. Gheevala, secretary, Indian Merchants' Chamber, letter, 9 January
1968. Some picture of the dominant position of non-Marhattas in the business
life of Bombay city may be seen from the list published by the IMC of the
persons who have served on its governing committee between 1907, when it
was founded, and 1967; *Diamond Jubilee Souvenir* (Bombay, 1967). There are
other chambers of commerce in Bombay city, but the IMC is the largest, the
most representative of big business, and the most powerful. The relationship
between the IMC and the Bombay Citizens' Committee was a close one. The
president of the Citizens' Committee, Pushottamdas Thakurdas, was several
times president of the IMC and was a member of its committee for thirty-four
years. Four of the six vice-presidents of the Citizens' Committee served on the
committee of the IMC for an average of fourteen years.

"It may be safely asserted that the bulk of the capital invested in the different industrial enterprises [in Bombay city] has mainly come from Parsis, Gujaratis, Bhatias [from Saurashtra and Kutch], and several other communities." The city's prosperity is "largely the result of non-Maharashtrian effort and enterprise." [55]

"It is not an uncommon experience that with new boundaries based on linguistic affinity, trade in the hands of minorities has a tendency to be seriously jeopardized." [56]

"As the language of business on which rests the economic structure of the city, Marathi has no place in Bombay." The argument that the city was "built by the labor of the working classes of Maharashtra and therefore they should be the masters of the city" is "novel," and "futile and invalid." [57]

Arguments such as these, D. R. Gadgil wrote, were "of a type which even European capitalists no longer dare to put forward in relation to their more genuine work of development . . . in the Asiatic countries." [58] Indeed, to Lalji Pendse, a leftist leader of the samiti and its historian, the Samyukta Maharashtra movement was analogous to an anticolonial movement against the capitalists-imperialists of Bombay city, who happened to be Gujaratis, and who had turned Maharashtra into a colony which supplied their metropolis with raw materials, labor, and markets.[59]

The leftist leaders of the Samyukta Maharashtra Samiti found it more to their ideological taste to view the struggle for Bombay city as a class conflict rather than a sectarian struggle among "communalists." [60] Accordingly, they were inclined to present their movement as one for working- and middle-class liberation from the clutches of "vested interests." Yet it seems clear that their reliance was on linguistic, Marathi, rather than on communally undifferentiated lower classes.

55. Bombay Citizens' Committee, *Memorandum*.
56. Gujarat PCC, *Memorandum Submitted to the States Reorganization Commission* (Ahmadabad, 1954).
57. Mahagujarat Parishad, *Formation of Maha Gujarat: A Memorandum Submitted to the States Reorganization Commission* (Vallabh Vidyanagar, 1954).
58. Samyukta Maharashtra Parishad, *Reorganization of States*, p. 65.
59. Interview, Bombay, 27 April 1967.
60. According to S. M. Joshi, one of the reasons the Praja Socialist party's national executive at first hesitated to become involved in the samiti was that it considered the Samyukta Maharashtra movement a "parochial" one; interview, 4 April 1967.

The proposal, made several times, for a plebiscite in Bombay city to determine its political future was rejected by the Samyukta Maharashtra Parishad and the Maharashtra PCC. The proposal, the parishad wrote, was "no more than a palpable ruse" of those who "proceed on the expectation that the large new and old floating population of Bombay [city] which consists largely of speakers of languages other than Marathi would vote against the incorporation of Bombay in Maharashtra." [61] It is difficult not to conclude that those who rejected a plebiscite did so because they proceeded on the same expectation.

B. S. Hiray, the leading Maharashtrian Congressman in 1956 and chief minister-presumptive of Maharashtra, was only willing to accept a plebiscite after a brief "three-unit" interregnum, if during the interregnum Maharashtra's capital was established at Bombay city. To establish the state's government anywhere else would necessarily reduce the number and influence of Marathi-speakers eligible to vote in the plebiscite. Some of Hiray's colleagues, however, were unwilling to agree to a plebiscite under any circumstances.[62] They feared that the Marhatta population of the city, which had been steadily declining over the years, from 51 percent in 1931 to 44 percent in 1951, could be further reduced by discriminatory hiring practices. T. R. Naravene, the leader of the dissident Congress Jana Parishad, claimed that there was a letter in circulation advising the city's industrialists to reduce their hirings of Marhatta labor.[63] They feared that "the intellectual proletariat from outside Maharashtra," that is, south Indians, apprehensive "that their chances of employment in Bombay may be jeopardized, if Bombay forms a part of Maharashtra," would vote against Samyukta Maharashtra if a plebiscite were held.[64] The samiti claimed a particular triumph in the legislative assembly by-election victory on 14 November 1957 of V. R. Tulla, a south Indian and a Samyukta Maharashtra supporter, from the "cosmopolitan" Nagpada constituency in the city. But the

61. Samyukta Maharashtra Parishad, *Reorganization of States*, p. 74. The last suggestion for a plebiscite, met by resignation threats from the Maharashtra PCC, was made by Nehru in his announcement of a "three-unit" formula on 3 June 1956.

62. Letter dated 11 January 1956 and reproduced in Deogirikar, *Twelve Years in Parliament*, p. 204.

63. *Free Press Journal*, 14 July 1956. Babubhai Chinai, a prominent Gujarati businessman from the city and a Congress M.P., denied this.

64. Gadgil, D. R., *The Future of Bombay City* (Bombay: Samyukta Maharashtra Parishad, n.d.), p. 29.

contribution of south Indian sentiments for Samyukta Maharashtra to his victory is by no means clear. It may be assumed that many south Indians voted for him because he is a south Indian, and Nagpada is in an area (Ward E) with a relatively low percentage of Gujaratis and a relatively high percentage of Marhattas. In other constituencies where there are relatively high concentrations of south Indians, such as Colaba (Ward A) and Chembur (Ward M), Congress had done well in the 1957 general elections,[65] and those who opposed Samyukta Maharashtra also claimed support from south Indians.[66]

A "new synthesis" among lower-class groups in Bombay city seems no more to have taken place than a "new synthesis" among the caste groups of Maharashtra. Militant Maharashtrianism in Bombay city has been captured in recent years by a new organization, Shiv Sena. Founded in 1966 by Bal Thackeray, a well-known political cartoonist and the son of a famous anti-Brahman journalist, Shiv Sena has made its peace with the "vested interests," Gujarati and other, and it directs its animus and its violence against south Indian workers and small merchants whom it accuses of taking jobs away from Marhattas and increasing the city's crime rate.[67] The "vested interests" look at Shiv Sena and say "our apprehensions . . . have been amply supported by subsequent events." [68] But they have come to terms with "Maratha Raj" and business goes on as usual. The issue of Bombay city is closed.

65. *Census of India*, 1961, vol. 10, part 10 (1-B), Greater Bombay Census Tables, p. 185. Needless to say, anyone interested in the *actual* support for the samiti among south Indians in the general elections and subsequent by-elections would have to make a more thorough investigation than this. But such an investigation is beyond the scope of this study.

66. C. C. Shah in *Lok Sabha Debates*, vol. 10, part 2, 14 December 1955; and K. K. Shah, former president, Bombay PCC, interview, New Delhi, 25 May 1967.

67. This shift from "class war" to "race war" happened most dramatically during the by-election campaign in the spring of 1967 for the Lok Sabha seat from northeast Bombay city. The Sampoorna Maharashtra Samiti, the Samyukta Maharashtra Samiti's rump, supported the independent candidacy of former defense minister and *ancien terrible* of the Congress left, V. K. Krishna Menon. Shiv Sena supported the Congress candidate, who is a Maharashtrian, and opposed Krishna Menon because he is a south Indian. Krishna Menon lost. Shiv Sena received much of the credit for his defeat, and Congress received the condemnation for accepting the support of the "communal" and "fascistic" Shiv Sena. See E. Balasubramaniam, "Shiv Sena: Child of Congress," *Swarajya*, 27 May 1967, and *Enlite*, 1 April 1967, pp. 4–8.

68. C. L. Gheevala, letter.

The movement for Mahagujarat, a single unilingual Gujarati state, developed as a reaction to the movement for Samyukta Maharashtra. The Gujarat PCC and its allies who dominated the testimony presented to the States Reorganization Commission on behalf of Gujarat argued in favor of the retention of the multilingual status quo. Only in the event of Bombay's dissolution did they ask for a Gujarati state, enlarged by the addition of Kutch and Saurashtra, neither with any significant separatist ambitions, and certain areas on its border with Maharashtra.

In their identical memoranda to the States Reorganization Commission, the Gujarat PCC and the Gujarat Sima Samiti (Gujarat Boundary Association), followed the line laid down by the Dar Commission and the JVP Committee. They acknowledged that "consideration has to be given to linguistic homogeniety." But they emphasized that such consideration "should not be the sole or even principal criterion" for reorganization, and "must be set against economic and administrative considerations." Then, with their eyes no doubt turned toward the Marhattas, they particularly warned against any reorganization which "has for its inspiration the revival of medieval particularism with all its attendent ambitions [for] regional aggrandizement." [69]

The Marhatta ambition which most concerned those who testified for Gujarat was the ambition for Bombay city. "Before the growth of the movement for Samyukta Maharashtra," they contended, "the Maharashtrians claimed only Poona as their political, intellectual, and cultural capital, as indeed it is." [70]

Although there were Gujarati politicians who viewed multilingual Bombay, twice the size of Mahagujarat, as a pasture large enough to feed great ambition, few Gujaratis, businessmen or Congressmen, were enamored of the status quo as such and absolutely preferred it to having a state of their own. There was much to be said in favor of a state of one's own.[71] But Gujaratis, in general, simply did not

69. *Memorandum to the States Reorganization Commission* (Ahmadabad, 1954). The Sima Samiti was an ad hoc "citizens' group" auxiliary of the Gujarat Congress. Composed of lawyers, academics, and businessmen, its primary concern was staking out the borders of a possible Gujarat state. See also the memorandum submitted by H. V. Divatia on behalf of the Gujarat Sahitya Parishad (Gujarat Literary Society), Bombay, 1954.

70. Ibid.

71. Interviews and K. P. Mukerji and S. Ramaswami, *Reorganization of Indian States* (Bombay: Popular Book Depot, 1956)

feel as intensely about it as did the Marhattas. And those who spoke on their behalf were unwilling to give up Bombay city in order to gain Mahagujarat. If the Marhattas wanted Samyukta Maharashtra, the Gujarat PCC resolved at Mehamadabad in October 1955, then *they* would have to sacrifice Bombay city. The "three-unit" division was the only solution. A solution, it might be added, which would allow the Gujaratis to have their cake and eat it too: a Gujarat state and a separate Bombay city run by Gujaratis.

Only a small group, the Mahagujarat Parishad, significant primarily as the precursor of the Mahagujarat movement, made a case before the States Reorganization Commission in favor of the creation of a unilingual state in preference to the maintenance of the status quo. It solved the Bombay city problem by claiming that in the coastal taluks of Thana district "as far [south] as Bombay city" the spoken language was either the "standard form of Gujarati" or a Gujarati dialect mixed with Konkani, "a language fundamentally different from Marathi." [72] Therefore, since the language borders of Gujarat were contiguous with Bombay city, Bombay city should be the capital of Mahagujarat.

Whatever the linguistic affinities of Konkani may be, however, and the Maharashtrians called it "a mere dialect of Marathi," [73] the Congress-Government elite has consistently preferred to draw boundaries by the art of politics rather than the science of linguistics. And through no art or science could they have convinced the Marhattas to accept Bombay city as the capital of Gujarat. The Mahagujarat Parishad's claim on the city was never seriously considered — even, one suspects, by the parishad, which would have settled for "three units." [74]

In August 1956 Ahmadabad had its teeth set for becoming the capital of Mahagujarat. Then at the eleventh hour, without warning or consulting the Gujarat PCC, the "three-unit" formula was withdrawn from the States Reorganization Bill, and Ahmadabad discovered that it was to remain another provincial town in "big bilingual"

72. Mahagujarat Parishad, *Formation of Mahagujarat.*
73. Samyukta Maharashtra Parishad, *United Maharashtra*, p. 21.
74. Himatlal Shukla, the parishad's first president, interview, Ahmadabad, 28 April 1967. There was a linguistic-provincial organization which wanted a Konkani state made up of the coastal *taluks* in Thana, Kolaba, and Ratnagiri districts with Bombay city as its capital. Needless to say, it was ignored; Mukerji and Ramaswami interviews.

Bombay. New forces broke through the Congress surface, and old alignments cracked.

The movement for a single unilingual Gujarti state bore a striking resemblance to the Mahavidarbha movement. Like the Mahavidarbha movement after 1957, the Mahagujarat movement was largely a reaction to Congress-Government elite concessions to the Marhattas. As the linguistic-provincial movement in Nag-Vidarbha was galvanized by the fear of losing a capital city, so the Mahagujarat movement was stimulated by the prospect of gaining one. Although the Mahagujarat movement reached into the countryside for support, it was rooted in Ahmadabad. Its supporters, like the supporters of Mahavidarbha, were a heterogeneous group. The three major nonparty groups in the movement, all concentrated in Ahmadabad city and its hinterland, the surrounding districts of Ahmadabad, Kaira, and Mehsana, were landholding farmers, students, and businessmen. It had two associational manifestations: the Mahagujarat Janata Parishad (People's Party) and the Nagarik Paksha (Citizens' Party) of Ahmadabad city.

In preparation for the first general elections in 1952, rightist Independents and former Congressmen, and groups known generically as the Khedut Sangh (Peasants' Association) had mobilized peasant proprietors in several districts of Gujarat, including those surrounding Ahmadabad, against the Bombay Land Tenancy Act of 1948. The Khedut Sangh parties dissolved after their poor performance in the elections, but landholding peasants and their leaders were obvious recruits for a movement in 1957 which promised to put land reform legislation in the hands of "their" government. "The Rightist elements which opposed the Congress in 1952, joined the [Mahagujarat] Janata Parishad in 1957." [75]

Two things should be noted about peasant proprietors' support for the Mahagujarat movement. First, it was largely divorced from the caste politics, as such, of Gujarat; that is, the internal struggle for power and position among castes.[76] There were, to be sure, politicians with large caste followings who led them into the movement, men like Bhailalbhai Patel in Kaira district and Purshottam-

75. D. N. Pathak et al., *Three General Elections in Gujarat* (Ahmadabad: Gujarat University, 1966).
76. For this, see Rajni Kothari and Rushikesh Maru, "Caste and Secularism in India," *Journal of Asian Studies* 25 (November 1965): 33–50.

das Patel in Mehsana. But the "upsurge [for Mahagujarat] took on the character of a mass movement based on solidarities that cut across party and caste." [77] Second, although landholding farmers provided the movement with the majority of its electoral strength, the movement's leadership was leftist or urban or both.

Students have been involved in linguistic movements all over India. The desire of Indian students to think and read and write and learn in their own languages has deep psychological and sociological roots; but it is perhaps sufficient for our purposes to note that under the Indian constitution education is primarily a state rather than a central responsibility, and that education is the key to middle-class employment in an employers' market. The students of Ahmadabad were the instigators and the shock troops of the Mahagujarat movement.

On 8 August 1956, after the withdrawal of the "three-unit" formula had been confirmed, a large group of students marched to Congress House in Ahmadabad to protest. There was violence and police firing. Some students were killed and others were wounded. Then there was more violence and more firing. To make matters worse, the firing by police serving an Indian government coincided with the fourteenth anniversary celebration among the Ahmadabad students of the shooting of a nationalist student by police serving a British government. A commission of inquiry, the Kotval Commission, appointed two years later concluded that the 1956 "disturbances broke out spontaneously because of a sense of frustration and shock among the people in Ahmadabad as a result of the denial to them of a separate state of Gujarat and the firing at the Congress House." [78]

Student groups formed and there were disturbances in other cities in Gujarat, but the main force of the storm and the center of the movement remained in Ahmadabad. Under the leadership of Harihar Khambolja, a law student, the students formed the Mahagujarat Vidyarthi Samiti (Students' Committee) and controlled the movement for about a month. By September the politicians had taken over the movement's leadership: Praja Socialists, Communists, dissi-

77. Ibid. See also A. H. Somjee, *Voting Behavior in an Indian Village* (Baroda: Department of Political Science, M. S. University of Baroda, 1959), and interviews.

78. Government of Bombay, *Report of the Commission of Inquiry (Shri Justice S. P. Kotval) on the Cases of Police Firing at Ahmadabad on the 12th, 13th, and 14th August 1958.*

dent Congressmen, and some Khedut Sanghis. The association's name was changed to the Mahagujarat Janata Parishad, and Indulal Yajnik, an old Gandhian and a "pukka leftist" was elected president.[79]

Himatlal Shukla, a former president of the old Mahagujarat Parishad, was for a time an officer of the new Janata Parishad, but the new parishad was a different organization. Its leftist and student leaders, if not indifferent to Bombay city's fate, were unwilling to sacrifice Mahagujarat to keep the city from the Marhattas. The Janata Parishad had no organization in Bombay city, and little sympathy with its "vested interests," whom, like the Samyukta Maharashtra Samiti, they viewed as the stumbling block to linguistic reorganization. This difference became more and more manifest in the months following the second general elections, and the more manifest it became, the more alienated the Janata Parishad grew from the business supporters of Mahagujarat and other conservatives like Shukla.

The businessmen of Ahmadabad reacted sharply to losing their anticipated capital city and a government of their own. The "big bilingual" scheme was condemned by the Ahmadabad Millowners Association, the Gujarat Chamber of Commerce, and other commerical associations in Ahmadabad.[80] Ten days after the Congress Working Committee announced its approval of the "big bilingual" solution, the business-dominated Ahmadabad city Congress Committee, by a vote of thirteen to four, denounced it and, in effect, dissolved itself into the Nagarik Paksha. Under the leadership of a prominent businessman, Chinubhai Chimanlal Seth, and in inharmonious cooperation with the Janata Parishad, the Nagarik Paksha took up the reins of municipal government in Ahmadabad.

Businessmen of Ahmadabad wanted a state capital of their own for the same general reasons that the businessmen of Nagpur did: to be near the seat of political power and to have access to it. In addition, many of them had made speculative land purchases in expectation of the construction of new state government buildings, and the price of land plummeted with their expectations. For some the Mahagujarat movement seemed to provide an opportunity to strike

79. Indulal Yajnik, interview, New Delhi, 28 March 1967 and Harihar Khambolja, interview, Ahmadabad, 29 April 1967.

80. *Times of India*, 5 August 1956, and *Bombay Chronicle*, 8 August 1956.

a blow at the Congress-dominated INTUC (Indian National Trade Union Congress) unions in the textile industry which had remained under Congress discipline. Unlike the Janata Parishad, however, many businessmen, even after the 1957 elections and to the bitter end, demanded nothing less than the resurrection of the "three-unit" formula: a separate Gujarat and a separate Bombay city. In June 1957 the executive committee of the Ahmadabad city Janata Parishad, against Yajnik's advice, first threw down the gauntlet to the Nagarik Paksha by taking a stand against the "three-unit" formula.[81] For the leaders of the Janata Parishad, in general, the formula was at best not "a practical proposition," and at worst, it was a scheme of "the Congress and the capitalists for continuing the present set-up."[82]

The Mahagujarat movement had come to a boil quickly, but lacking both the popular and political support of the movement for Samyukta Maharashtra, it cooled with almost equal rapidity. In August 1957, in an attempt to revitalize the sagging Janata Parishad, Harihar Khambolja called upon the students of Ahmadabad to "peacefully persuade" people in the city to boycott all public transportation for a period of a few days. A year later, the Janata Parishad, unsuccessful in every by-election that it had fought and with its membership steadily declining, attempted to resuscitate itself once more by "direct action." It requested permission from the municipal government, controlled by its erstwhile ally the Nagarik Paksha, to erect a "martyrs' memorial" in front of Congress House to commemorate the police firing of two years earlier. Its request was denied; it erected the memorial in spite of this. The police removed it a few days later. And the alliance between left and right in the cause of Mahagujarat went down finally in a hail of brickbats and bullets.[83]

Swarnakars and Sarafs

Opposition to the Government of India's Gold Control Rules of 1963 was organized by *swarnakars* and *sarafs*. The former are working goldsmiths, the latter, retail jewelers, moneylenders, and bul-

81. *Free Press Journal*, 15 June 1957.
82. *Hindustan Standard*, 5 December 1957, and *Hitavada*, 10 August 1957.
83. *Bombay Chronicle*, 17 July 1957, and Government of Bombay, *Report of the Commission of Inquiry*.

lion merchants.[84] By way of introduction, their organizations might be compared with those of the linguistic-provincial movements in western India on two points. First, the associations of *swarnakars* and *sarafs* were independent organizations with no institutional ties to any political party or parties. In part, this independence was dictated by necessity. Unlike the Marhattas or Gujaratis, the *swarnakars* and *sarafs* are relatively small groups scattered throughout India. They cannot provide a coalition of opposition parties with a regional base, nor are they numerous enough to tempt opposition parties into a national coalition. In part, the *swarnakars*, in particular, and the *sarafs* chose to be independent.

Second, the movement for Samyukta Maharashtra was in no small measure successful because it had great organized mass support: from voters and demonstrators. The *swarnakars* and *sarafs* were in no small measure successful in their oppositional campaigns because they had great unorganized mass support: from consumers. Throughout the life of the "fourteen-carat rule" Indian consumers continued to buy "pure gold," smugglers continued to supply it to them, and its price continued to rise. In the *sona bazaars* of large cities, where official surveillance was officialy most present, there were thriving black markets in "pure gold." In Saurashtra a village elder stated categorically that in his village there was no gold control. The price of "pure gold," which was about Rs. 108 for ten grams when the "fourteen-carat rule" was instituted, was about Rs. 145 for ten grams when it was withdrawn. Indian families did not declare their nonornament gold and they did not buy gold bonds. In March 1963, after the deadline for the declaration of nonornament gold under the rules had expired, the chairman of the Gold Control Board acknowledged that declarations were "far below expectations," that "only a fraction of privately-held non-ornament gold [had] been declared."[85] The second gold bonds scheme, which was launched in October 1965 and was expected to bring in Rs. 1 billion in "pure gold," had by July 1966 netted about Rs. 71 million.[86]

The successful opposition of the *swarnakars* and *sarafs* to the

84. "Goldsmith" is a caste as well as an occupational designation. There are many goldsmith castes in India, only a proportion of whose members earn their livelihoods by following the hereditary caste occupation of goldsmithery. Those who do are called *swarnakars*.
85. *Free Press Journal*, 15 May 1963, and *Times of India*, 1 April 1963.
86. *Hindustan Times*, 30 July 1966.

Gold Control Rules must be viewed within the context of this massive, widespread, and unorganized noncompliance and noncooperation with the law. The final argument against the rules was not only that they had created great hardships for people in the gold trade, but that they had done so without accomplishing any of their aims; that because of noncompliance and noncooperation, the rules were costing the government and Congress more than they were gaining for them. For the government, they cost tax revenues which it would otherwise have garnered and administrative cost which it would otherwise have saved. For Congress, they cost votes which it would otherwise have received and energy which it would otherwise not have dissipated.

The *swarnakars* and *sarafs* did not organize this consumers' "movement." That was hardly necessary. But they were critically in complicity. If they did not encourage noncompliance and noncooperation, they facilitated them by continuing to make available, illegally, their goods and services and by pressuring the Finance Ministry, in effect, to make noncompliance and noncooperation easier and less risky.

In the gold trade, goldsmiths are by far the largest occupational group. According to the 1961 *Census of India* there are about half a million persons in India following the professions of gold- and silversmithery. Roughly half of these are *swarnakars*. But when this number is increased by adding the families of working goldsmiths, and those who are goldsmiths by caste but not by profession, the total is in the millions.[87] These millions include not only those who are dependent upon *swarnakars* — wives and children — but also those to whom *swarnakars* can turn for assistance — well-to-do, well-placed, and politically skilled kinsmen and caste fellows.

By and large, goldsmithery is a hereditary caste profession. Traditionally, goldsmiths have been self-employed artisans. They receive bullion from their customers, fashion it into ornaments, and earn their livings by charging for their labor. In towns and cities, however, many goldsmiths work as employees or contract workers for *sarafs*. Or, if they remain self-employed, they have *sarafs* for competitors.

Sarafs, who are located principally in towns and cities, are traditionally moneylenders and bullion merchants. But since most bul-

87. According to goldsmith spokesmen.

lion is purchased for jewelry, and much jewelry is pawned, it is only a short step from these occupations to the trade of retail jeweler. Many *sarafs*, particularly in larger urban areas, have become primarily or solely retail jewelers. As an employer of smiths, the *saraf* has the advantage, general to those who employ labor in India, of being in a buyer's market. As a competing retail jeweler the *saraf* is also advantaged. His advantages are those of entrepreneurship and relative wealth. Many *sarafs* maintain "showrooms" with stocks of various styles of sample pieces or ready-made ornaments; they take orders for elaborate ornaments whose fashioning requires the skills of different goldsmiths, and "guarantee" the purity of the gold in the ornaments sold against the day when they return in mortgage. The development of transportation facilities have extended these advantages beyond the town and city.

Often *sarafs* follow their occupation in the footsteps of their fathers. But as merchants, generally, they come from a variety of caste backgrounds. Not surprisingly, many of them are goldsmiths by caste. In some such cases, the "dealer-goldsmith" or members of his family continue to do the work of goldsmithery or continue to identify themselves as goldsmiths. In other cases, *sarafs* from goldsmith backgrounds, who in their march to entrepreneurship have left goldsmithery behind them, prefer to leave their backgrounds behind them as well. Goldsmith castes are generally low on caste hierarchies, and whereas goldsmiths are traditionally stereotyped as dishonest workmen,[88] *sarafs* picture themselves as "trustees" of people's wealth.

Another class of retail jewelers should be mentioned. This is a relatively small group of prosperous merchants whose shops are located in major cities and tourist centers such as Jaipur and Agra. Their trade, generally, is less in standard high-purity gold ornaments than in gems, gem-set, enameled, and elaborately fashioned jewelry, art objects, and antiques which they sell to tourists, resident foreigners, and wealthy Indians. The honorary secretary of their trade association refers to them as India's "top class of jewel-

---

88. Jamila Brij Bhushan, an expert admirer of the Indian goldsmiths' craft, says that the smiths themselves "are usually notoriously dishonest," and quotes proverbs and stories attesting to their dishonesty; *Indian Jewellery, Ornaments, and Decorative Designs* (Bombay: D. B. Taraporevala and Sons, 1964), p. 132. My distinct impression from numerous interviews and conversations is that this stereotype has wide currency and that *sarafs* attempt to use it to their advantage.

ers" and sharply distinguishes them from mere *sarafs*.[89] But there are other prosperous jewelers who deal in precious stones, and neither lend money nor sell bullion, who identify themselves as *sarafs*. The two occupations really shade into one another at a comparable level of prosperity, as do those of *swarnaker* and *saraf*, and the differences between them are less in what they do than in how they think of themselves and how they wish to be thought of.

Of all these groups only the "top class of jewelers" had a national trade association in January 1963 when the Gold Control Rules were promulgated. The All-India Jewellers Association, whose membership is limited to jewelers dealing in precious stones, was founded in the late 1950s. Along with their domestic business, the "top class of jewelers" are also involved in import and export trade. This brings them into contact with the Government of India, from whom they must secure the necessary licenses and permits, and their association was in part an outgrowth of this contact.[90] Among the *swarnakars* and *sarafs* there were hundreds of local and neighborhood trade and social associations. These were primarily located in the *sona bazaars* of urban centers, where concentrations of goldsmiths and *sarafs* confront each other and government. But there were no national, and few state- or even citywide associations, and apparently there was little awareness of the problems or even the existence of associations in the same trade from locality to locality. Even in Bombay city, one of the centers of the jewelry trade, there was no citywide association of *sarafs*. National associations developed in response to the Gold Control Rules. The *swarnakars* were the first to act.

It is difficult to say how many goldsmiths were hurt by the rules and how badly. Although Finance Minister Morarji Desai told the members of the Lok Sabha in February 1963 that an estimate of one million smiths and their dependents displaced by the rules was "very much exaggerated," [91] Anil Basu, a goldsmith leader, told them less than a year later that the rules had driven two million people from their "hereditary vocation" and that "more than two

---

89. Sultan Singh Backliwal, interview, New Delhi, 1 November 1966.

90. A parallel organization, the Gem and Jewellery Export Promotion Council, was founded in 1966 by members of the Jewellers Association, specifically to "support, protect, maintain, increase, and promote the export of gems and jewellery"; *Memorandum and Articles of Incorporation.*

91. *Lok Sabha Debates*, 3d series, vol. 12, 20 February 1963.

hundred artisans [had] ended their miserable life by committing suicide." [92] It is clear, however, that the problem of unemployment among the smiths had been underestimated by the Finance Ministry at the time of the rules' announcement,[93] and their plight became clearer and more an issue as time went on. But the estimates of that plight made by the Finance Ministry and the goldsmiths continued to vary widely.[94]

It is common knowledge that in spite of the rules many smiths continued to manufacture "pure gold" ornaments clandestinely, and were perhaps hurt less by the rules than by the inconvenience, harassment, and illegal costs involved in evading them. But there is no doubt that they were hurt. The great efforts which they expended on getting the rules annulled is testimony to this. They could not carry on their profession as they had in the past, and there was risk for them and for their customers in carrying it on illegally. The Finance Ministry was both overtly hostile to their trade and cavalier in its approach to providing them with "rehabilitation" and alternate employment. For example, at a meeting with goldsmiths Morarji Desai, an outspoken man, told them, among other things, that their trade was "all bunkum," a business which "thrived only on smuggled gold," and in which "nobody trusted anybody." His ultimate aim, he said, was to stop even the manufacture of fourteen-carat gold ornaments.[95] In answer to questions raised by smiths in Madras about alternate employment, Desai "asked them to contact the Madras government." [96] Of the groups in the gold trade, the *swarnakars* were the least affluent, the most dependent on a particular skill, and therefore the most vulnerable to unemployment and proletarianization.

The Akhil Bharatiya Swarnakar Sangh (All-India Goldsmith Workers Association) was founded in Delhi in February 1963, one

92. Statements Laid on the Table, petition no. 16, LT–3743/64.

93. Morarji Desai also said in February 1963 that because goldsmiths could still work with fourteen-carat gold and other metals there was "no reason why all, or even a majority of the goldsmiths should lose employment." *Finance Minister's Statement in the Lok Sabha on the 20th February 1963 Regarding the Gold Control Scheme.*

94. Contemporaneous with the above statement by Anil Basu was an estimate from T. T. Krishnamachari, Desai's successor, that 80 percent of the goldsmiths were continuing to work at their craft and a "very comprehensive" rehabilitation scheme was available to the rest.

95. *Times of India,* 12 May 1963.

96. *Hindu,* 22 January 1963.

month after the rules came into force, and was specifically for the purpose of fighting them. The organizers of the Swarnakar Sangh were the leaders of the Delhi Goldsmith Workers Union, and particularly its president, Sardar Jaswant Singh. A refugee from West Pakistan, Jaswant Singh was instrumental in 1954 in founding the Delhi Goldsmith Workers Union. The objectives of the union were to organize working goldsmiths against "exploitation" by the "capitalist class" of jewelers, and to pressure the government to extend certain discriminatory privileges to goldsmiths by designating them a "backward class." The union brought into one organization local, Bengali, Punjabi, and other goldsmiths who were resident in Delhi.

During January and February 1963, Jaswant Singh and his general secretary, Ram Kishan Das, traveled throughout India trying to convince goldsmiths to unite against the rules. On 16 and 17 February they convened the constituent meeting of the Swarnakar Sangh in Delhi. A printed invitation was sent out requesting "all the goldsmith organizations of India" to send delegates "so that we can acquaint the government and the public with our grievances." [97] In many cases the convenors did not know whether the organizations they invited even existed, and they simply addressed the invitations to goldsmith unions in care of particular towns and cities and hoped that they would be delivered and that delegates would come.[98] The rules had primed the goldsmiths for such a move. In various parts of India delegations and associations of goldsmiths were being formed to petition and protest. Approximately 150 delegates, primarily from north India and representing goldsmith associations in ten states, attended the meeting at which the sangh was formed.

The Swarnakar Sangh was created as a federation of federations. It is composed of representatives of state units, several of which its officers helped to create, and these state units are made up of representatives of the primary, direct membership local units. The organizational model was the Congress party. The primary units were expected to collect one rupee a year in dues from each member and to send about half of this to the state units, who in turn were expected to forward five paise per primary member to the Swarnakar Sangh. Voluntary contributions were solicited, often from *sarafs* and from

97. An All-India Conference of Goldsmith Workers, a circular letter in Hindi, n.d.
98. Jaswant Singh, interviews, October and November 1966.

the smiths' nonartisan caste fellows, to supplement the revenue that was received from these modest dues.

Perhaps the most significant organizational decision made by the founders of the Swarnakar Sangh was to keep their association purely a goldsmith organization, unaffiliated with any political party. The Delhi Goldsmith Workers Union disaffiliated with the Congress-led INTUC, and neither the Swarnakar Sangh nor its constituent units sought affiliation with any of the party-led trade union federations. For president of the constituent meeting, an honorary office bestowed on some important person, the convenors of the Swarnakar Sangh sought a member of parliament, regardless of party affiliation, who was by caste a goldsmith. After the office was refused by one Congressman and a Jan Sanghi, it was accepted by Bal Govind Verma, a Congress member of the Lok Sabha. Although Mr. Verma insisted that he was not a goldsmith by caste, the convenors were certain that he was, and that was sufficient for them.[99] Their working officers, the Swarnakar Sangh decided, did not have to be goldsmiths by profession, but did have to be from goldsmith castes. For president they chose Bhavanishankar Asharam Soni, a lawyer from Ahmadabad, and at their second meeting, held in Bombay in April, they elected Anil Basu from Calcutta, an accountant and a Revolutionary Socialist party activist, as general secretary. Both men are goldsmiths by caste.

During the first several months that followed the organization of the Swarnakar Sangh, goldsmiths staged a number of demonstrations in the capital and in other cities, including token fasts, shop-closings for which they solicited the support of *sarafs*, and a *dharna* of "fifteen thousand strong" in front of the prime minister's residence.[100]

The initial success of these demonstrations was to publicize the goldsmiths' distress and by doing so to garner widespread support among politicians of all persuasions for "the *lakhs* [hundreds of thousands] of innocent people who have been rendered destitute . . . by a few carefree strokes of the pen of an omnivorous Administration," and equally widespread disapproval of the government's failure to adequately "rehabilitate" these *lakhs*.[101] It

---

99. Bal Govind Verma, and Shankar Prasad Das, interviews, Delhi, November 1966.

100. Akhil Bharatiya Swarnakar Sangh, *Whither Gold Control?* (Calcutta, n.d.)

101. Ibid.

was on the issue of "rehabilitation," loans to go into other businesses, job training, and alternate employment, that the Finance
Ministry was most open to attack. The ministry's failure to accurately gauge the extent and cost of a "rehabilitation" program that
would be sufficiently generous to keep the smiths from swelling the
already ample ranks of the unemployed put it on the defensive. Although the *swarnakars* were far less interested in being "rehabili-
tated" than in returning to their tools, it was on this issue that they
made their major thrust, and secured the important victory of having the "fourteen-carat rule" modified.[102]

In August 1963, T. T. Krishnamachari reentered the Union Cabinet
as finance minister. Desai's exit via the "Kamaraj Plan" was hailed
as a "big victory" at a meeting of the Swarnakar Sangh,[103] and
closely followed the beginning of the sangh's agitational activities
and Congress's defeat in three "prestige" parliamentary by-elections
in which the rules had been at issue. Presumably in response to
these events, at least in part, Krishnamachari announced as one of
his first acts a partial relaxation of the "fourteen-carat rule." Admit-
ting that the "fringe of the problem" of rehabilitating the smiths
had "hardly been touched," he declared that "pending the long
term process of rehabilitation," and only "for the time being" self-
employed goldsmiths would be permitted to *remake* high purity
gold ornaments into new ornaments of equally high purity.

    This concession, extended only to self-employed artisans, had a
profound effect on the Gold Control Rules and the relationship between goldsmiths and *sarafs*. It fatally undermined the "fourteen-
carat rule," which according to all three finance ministers who
served between 1963 and 1966, including Krishnamachari, was the

102. Ibid., and various memoranda published in Hindi. By December 1964,
of the estimated 270,000 goldsmiths in India 217,000 had chosen to become
"certified goldsmiths" under the rules, amendments of September 1963, and
they were therefore ineligible for rehabilitation benefits, *Lok Sabha Debates*, 3d
series, vol. 37, 21 December 1964. In Delhi, by September 1964, only 711 of
the estimated 5,000 goldsmiths had sought alternate jobs through employment
exchanges in which they were supposedly accorded preferential treatment. Of
the Rs. 800,000 authorized for "rehabilitation" in Delhi, Rs. 270,000 were
spent; Ibid., vol. 33, 10 September 1964. In Delhi, according to Jaswant Singh,
the smiths who availed themselves of "rehabilitation" services were principally
those who were unemployed or underemployed before the rules came into
being.
103. *Express*, 26 August 1963.

key provision of the rules.[104] Gold ornaments are made by smiths in thousands of villages, in tiny shops in the bazaars of hundreds of towns and cities, and, if need be, they can be (and were) made in the homes of customers. Who would be able to say whether a new "pure gold" bangle, for example, had been refashioned from an old, legally undeclared ornament or from a new, illegally undeclared "biscuit" of smuggled gold? In short, the "fourteen-carat concession" to self-employed artisans facilitated the further evasion of the rules.

It is probable, as the *sarafs* charged, that the "fourteen-carat concession" diverted a good part of what ornament-making business there was away from them and directly to the artisans. For the leaders of the Swarnakar Sangh, the concession, therefore, was not only a victory against the government but an unexpected triumph over their old "exploiters," the jewelers. For the concession, the sangh wrote, Krishnamachari "binds the Indian goldsmith . . . in gratitude." [105] From this point on the approach of the sangh's leaders to gold control became more complex: they continued to want those regulations which adversely affected the smiths annulled, but they now also began to want those regulations which gave them an advantage over the *sarafs* retained, and if possible augmented. They were wary. There was no disposition to see the finance minister as a friend, but they began to see his worth as an enemy's enemy.

It was characteristic of the big-city oriented leadership of the Swarnakar Sangh, people like Jaswant Singh, to view the *saraf* as an enemy — an exploitative employer and an advantaged competitor. It was this view which tended to shape the sangh's demands, particularly after the "fourteen-carat concession."

Following the lead of the Delhi Goldsmith Workers Union, the Swarnakar Sangh suggested in its first resolution that smuggling should be reduced not by punishing goldsmiths but by having gov-

104. It is unlikely that Krishnamachari, a firm supporter of gold control, purposely undermined the rules. More than a year after the concession, in answer to the demand for a complete annulment of the "fourteen-carat rule" he said, "If the fourteen-carat rule is abrogated there would be no reduction in the demand for gold and the position would be the same as without gold control." *Lok Sabha Debates,* 3d series, vol. 37, 21 December 1964.

105. Akhil Bharatiya Swarnakar Sangh, "Supplementary Memorandum to the Joint Committee of Parliament on the Gold (Control) Bill of 1963" (mimeographed).

ernment agencies buy gold at the international price and supply it directly to the artisans. "The right to make jewellery should be given to the artisan, the right to order it should only be given to the customer, and permission to keep stocks of jewellery should not be given." [106] In other words, the *saraf* should be eliminated from the gold trade: as a bullion merchant, a contractor, and a retail jeweler.

In the early stages of their battle against the rules, however, the Swarnakar Sangh was inclined to treat the *sarafs* as allies in a common cause. In its pamphlet *Whither Gold Control?* published in English a month before the "fourteen-carat concession," the sangh restated its demands but did not suggest again that the government put the *sarafs* out of business. It was only after the "fourteen-carat concession" that this suggestion became an integral part of the goldsmiths' demands. At its Jaipur meeting in April 1964, the Swarnakar Sangh called upon the government to reorganize the gold trade as *swarna-silpa*, gold handicrafts: an industry composed of self-employed artisans whose raw materials would be supplied by the government and whose product would be sold by the government in India and abroad. At its subsequent meetings this demand was reiterated, and the related demand for the complete abrogation of the "fourteen-carat rule" crystallized into the demand for complete abrogation of the "fourteen-carat rule" *for goldsmiths*.[107]

Swarna-silpa was the panacea of urban, class-conscious goldsmith leaders. But outside Bombay and Delhi and Calcutta, in smaller provincial towns, goldsmiths and jewelers, though divided by class differences — employee and employer, poor and rich, artisan and entrepreneur — are not infrequently bound together by common ties of artisanship, caste, and family.

Rajkot is a city of about two hundred thousand in Saurashtra, now part of Gujarat. In 1963 it attracted considerable attention when the Congress candidate in a parliamentary by-election was defeated by the Swatantra party leader M. R. Masani. It was widely believed that popular resentment against the rules, organized by goldsmiths and *sarafs*, played a major part in Congress's defeat in what had been regarded as one of its strongholds.

Many of the jewelers of Rajkot are goldsmiths by caste and many

106. Memorandum, Hindi, n.d., and Goldsmith Workers Union, Delhi, resolution no. 1, n.d.
107. B. A. Soni, interview, Ahmadabad, 19 January 1967.

of them were artisans in the recent past. Under the rules they are "licensed dealers," but much of their work is done by family members who are "certified goldsmiths." Many are members of the local goldsmiths' organization as well as members of the association of local *sarafs*.

The owners of Khushaldas Dayalji and Sons, the largest jewelry store in Rajkot, stopped working as artisans less than ten years ago, and they identify themselves with the goldsmiths of their own caste rather than local *sarafs* who come from a different caste background. Manilal Rugnath Rampara is a goldsmith of their caste. He comes from their village and they are kinsmen. Manilal is a working goldsmith, although like Jaswant Singh in Delhi he is a goldsmith-politician and his political activities frequently take him away from his tools. He was the president of the Rajkot Chandi Karigar Mandal (Silversmiths' Association) and the Akhil Gujarat Swarnakar Sangh and a vice-president of the Akhil Bharatiya Swarnakar Sangh.

While seated in Khushaldas Dayalji's "showroom" and surrounded by its obviously well-to-do proprietors, Manilal was elaborate and scathing in his denunciation of *sarafs'* "exploitation" of artisans. But they had heard all this before, and they were content that Manilal, no supporter of *swarna-silpa*, was not talking about them. Manilal's enmity, an enmity which they shared, was directed toward the "big bosses" of the gold trade in Bombay and Delhi, who did not come to the jeweler's profession through the route of artisanship and goldsmith caste background.[108] But this was a distant and largely an ideological enmity.[109] The issue at hand was the rules, a burden on both *swarnakars* and *sarafs* of Rajkot. The ties that bound them together may not have been love, but they were sufficient to the task of uniting them against the rules and in favor of Masani. Manilal's real enmity was for those who "are not with us," and "us" included the vice-president of the Rajkot Chandi Karigar

108. The following incident is perhaps an illustration of the different perspectives of the sangh's national and local leadership. I was directed to Khushaldas Dayalji and Sons by the general secretary of the All-India Sarafa Association, B. Mahajan, who is no more an admirer of the leaders of the sangh than they are of him. B. A. Soni, the president of the sangh, directed me to Manilal. When I arrived in Rajkot, Manilal and the owners of Khushaldas Dayalji were together in the latter's showroom, and some of my interviewing was conducted under these completely cordial circumstances.

109. Ironically, it may be less distant and ideological for Khushaldas Dayalji, which has a branch in Bombay city, than for Manilal.

Mandal, a Brahman jeweler who was, of course, neither by caste nor by calling a goldsmith.

Manilal's solicitude for jewelers from goldsmith backgrounds was not entirely lacking among the urban leaders of the Swarnakar Sangh. B. A. Soni, the president of the sangh, displayed a certain tolerance for jewelers like Khushaldas Dayalji that he did not have for the "big guns" of the gold trade, jewelers who do not know "ABC" about artisanship. But the importance of this solicitude should not be exaggerated. There was certainly never any inclination, for example, even before the sangh's program crystallized, to bring sarafs who were goldsmiths by caste into leadership positions within the organization, although several would have jumped at the opportunity.[110] Both the process of fission which has traditionally created new groups from old ones and the process of fusion which has more recently brought groups together in new formations have taken place for the urban goldsmith in the secular context of class conflict between goldsmith-artisans and goldsmith-jewelers. Ties of caste and family, of course, remain. But the leaders of the sangh were primarily concerned with protecting the goldsmiths as a class of artisans, and securing advantages for them against the sarafs as a class, and it was clearly toward these ends that their program, particularly swarna-silpa, was directed.

It was as a direct result of the "fourteen-carat concession" to self-employed goldsmiths that the sarafs formed a national organization. Largely on the initiative of the All-Delhi Sarafa Association and its president, Mali Ram Hira, the All-India Sarafa Association was founded in Delhi in November 1963. Its constituent meeting was timed to coincide with the discussion in Parliament of the Gold (Control) Bill of 1963, a measure adopted by the government on Krishnamachari's urging to put the rules on a permanent footing. The Sarafa Association elected as its president and general secretary well-to-do jewelers from Delhi and Bombay.

B. Mahajan, the general secretary and the leading figure in the association, came into the jewelry business when his elder brother, who was to take over the family firm, died. At that time he was

110. A common complaint among smiths was that jewelers kept trying to take over their organizations. Jaswant Singh said this had happened to the Delhi Prant Sonar Sabha (Delhi Province Goldsmiths Association), a goldsmith caste organization.

studying for an advanced degree in sociology at Edinburgh University. His qualification for high office was not his political experience — he had none — but, he thinks, his education. He was someone who could write "grammatical English," a talent put to good use in a number of pamphlets published by the Sarafa Association. Between 1963 and 1966, Mahagan estimated that he spent about half his time on association business, including forty thousand miles of travel throughout India. During these travels he helped organize over 350 local associations of bullion merchants, jewelers, moneylenders, and pawnbrokers into statewide associations and to federate these into the national Sarafa Association.[111]

In its official propaganda, the Sarafa Association said nothing of the *swarnakars'* demands for *swarna-silpa*. But in private conversations the expressions of jewelers and *sarafs* ranged from tolerant condescension to outrage. The smiths, according to their lights, were guilty of gross ingratitude. They had become "cheats." When the smiths had come to them and asked them to close their shops for a day in February 1963 to protest against the rules, the *sarafs* had closed them.[112] When the smiths had come to them and begged for money, they had given it. According to B. Mahajan, the jewelers of Bombay city had collected Rs. 60,000 for the relief of goldsmiths. But when the finance minister announced his "arbitrary and discriminatory" concession, the smiths had grabbed for it and their "communistic" leaders [113] asked the government to turn the *sarafs* out of the gold trade.

The Swarnakar Sangh's dislike for jewelers, coupled with the Sarafa Association's resentment against the sangh's ready acceptance of the "fourteen-carat concession" and its demand for *swarna-silpa*, precluded cooperation between the two associations against the rules. But even between the Sarafa Association and the association of "top jewelers," the All-India Jewellers Association, cooperation was minimal, although they shared not only an aversion to the rules but also an objection to the "fourteen-carat concession." The honorary secretary of the Jewellers Association attributed this to the *sarafs'* "inferiority complex" and their practice of making tactical deci-

111. B. Mahajan, interview, Bombay, 3 January 1967. Mahajan reported that only in Andhra and Madras were there statewide units before the Gold Control Rules.

112. Not in Delhi, however, according to sangh leaders.

113. A epithet applied most frequently to Anil Basu.

sions without first consulting the Jewellers Association. Mali Ram Hira, speaking for the Sarafa Association, explained it with a shrug: "In India, everyone wants to be a leader." [114]

The oppositional tactics of the jewelers and *sarafs* differed considerably from those employed by the Swarnakar Sangh. Jewelers and *sarafs* generally eschewed extraparliamentary agitation as an oppositional tactic. When the goldsmiths, who agitated periodically and frequently between 1963 and 1966, first began their "direct action" campaign, individual *sarafs* were willing to cooperate or contribute money to help them. But few *sarafs* were willing to go out into the streets to shout slogans and carry placards. Considerations of status prevented them from doing this. *Sarafs* are, after all, "businessmen," "established people" with a "long tradition of being lawabiding . . . citizens." [115] Although they were sure that all the finance ministers were hostile to them, they claimed to have the ears of important people in high places, including the Union Cabinet. Personal appeals to these important friends and customers was the oppositional style preferred by the Jewellers Association, and the Sarafa Association, with the assistance of a conservative, professional public relations organization, embarked on a publicity campaign against the rules.[116] Only in August and September of 1966, when the goldsmiths massed in Delhi in protest against the rules, did the Sarafa and Jewellers associations take out processions of their own. But these were almost unnoticeable sideshows next to the thousands of smiths gathered in front of Parliament House chanting while Anil Basu embarked on an "indefinite" fast. The Jewellers Association's "procession" hardly qualifies for the name. On 29 August about eighty well-dressed jewelers, carrying placards professionally lettered in English, met with Prime Minister Indira Gandhi for about fifteen minutes, deposited a memorandum with her in which

114. Interview, Delhi, 26 October 1966.
115. Sultan Singh Backliwal and Mali Ram Hira, interviews. See also Delhi Jewellers Association, *Memorandum*, 29 August 1966.
116. A confrontation between the "top jewelers" and Morarji Desai when he was finance minister was described with particular annoyance by the honorary secretary of the Jewellers Association. Desai, it seems, was flipping through the pages of a copy of *Shankar's Weekly* when the delegation of jewelers was led into his office, and he continued to do so without so much as looking up or inviting them, "the Tiffanys, Cartiers, and Van Cleefs and Arpels of India," to take seats.

they complained of being discriminated against by the "fourteen-carat concession," had their photograph taken, and peacefully departed.

Although some goldsmith associations placed high hopes in the "fourteen-carat concession," it became increasingly clear that these hopes were not to be realized. As late as 1966 the Madurai Certified Goldsmiths Association passed a resolution in which they asked the government not to annul the rules but to further amend them in favor of the smiths. The association's president was quoted as saying that the smiths were better off making new ornaments out of old ones than they had been when they were working for jewelers.[117] But according to B. A. Soni, the concession had restored only about 25 percent of the goldsmiths' business, was of little aid to the artisans who had previously worked for jewelers, and was causing "ill feelings" among them for the self-employed artisans who had benefited most from it.[118] Therefore, although the Swarnakar Sangh had welcomed the concession, it had proved inadequate and was threatening its internal cohesion. Too, the sangh's leaders shared the jewelers' suspicions that the concession was largely an attempt by the government to blunt the gold trade's attack on the rules by setting smiths and *sarafs* against each other. *Swarna-silpa* would have to wait. As one goldsmith leader put it, "First we must defeat the government, then we will handle the *sarafs*." [119] By 1966 this had become the sangh's order of priorities and it reestablished, however tenuously, a united front in the gold trade against the rules.

In their testimony before the Joint Committee on the Gold (Control) Bill of 1963, spokesmen for smiths and *sarafs*, without minimizing their differences, stressed the primacy of their mutual opposition to the rules. In response to leading questions from the few Congress advocates of the bill on the committee, B. A. Soni agreed that goldsmiths were exploited by *sarafs,* but he finally answered this line of questioning by saying, "Is it the intention of Government that we [goldsmiths and *sarafs*] should fight amongst ourselves? We do not want to fight amongst ourselves." "We are not against goldsmiths," the spokesman for the Greater Bombay Jewellers and Bullion Dealers Association told the Committee. "Why split

117. *Hindu,* 28 June 1966.
118. Interview.
119. Interview, January 1967.

up the business and separate them [goldsmiths and *sarafs*] and pitch them one against the other?" [120]

According to leaders of the Akhil Bharatiya Swarnakar Sangh, by 1967 their organization had so penetrated the countryside that village goldsmiths were as well organized against the rules as those in towns and cities. The membership figure which they invariably gave for the sangh and its affiliated state and local groups was two million, and with dependents, ten million.[121] Fantastic figures! The actual number of members and how deeply the goldsmiths' associations penetrated the countryside, which in many cases was barely penetrated by the rules, is unknown to me and, I suspect, to the leaders of the sangh as well. What is known, however, is impressive. In a few short years the Swarnakar Sangh and its affiliated units with their own leadership were able to organize relatively unpoliticized, unorganized, and scattered agglomerations of goldsmith groups which shared only a common vocation and a common anxiety into a national interest association. Further, they were able to monopolize the goldsmiths' struggle against the rules, to retain that monopoly throughout the struggle, and to win. They organized meetings in various parts of India and agreed upon a common program. They organized and coordinated lobbying campaigns and demonstrations in various cities. Their final demonstration in front of Parliament House and elsewhere in September 1966 ended only with the government's promise to annul completely the "fourteen-carat rule."

Some measure of the Swarnakar Sangh's hold on the goldsmiths' opposition to the rules can be taken from the testimony presented to the joint committee of Parliament. Goldsmith associations from almost every state and every large city testified. With the possible exception of only one, they were all affiliates of the sangh and they spoke with one voice against the rules and the bill. Some submitted original memoranda, but added to them a statement of their support for the sangh.[122] Others merely duplicated, entirely or in large part, the sangh's memoranda.[123] In his eleventh hour defense of the

120. Lok Sabha Secretariat, *Joint Committee on the Gold (Control) Bill 1963: Evidence* (September 1964).

121. B. A. Soni and Jaswant Singh, interviews.

122. For example, Shri Gujarat Suvarnakar Sangh, Madhya Pradesh Swarnakar Sangh, Tamilaha [Madras] Viswakarma Central Sangham.

123. For example, Maharashtra Pradesh Swarnakar Sangh, Bangiya [West

rules, Sachindra Chaudhuri, Krishnamachari's successor at the Finance Ministry, complained that "the *swarnakars* from one part of
India make one demand the *swarnakars* from another part of India
make another demand." [124] This is not the evidence of the public
record.[125]

With the withdrawal of the "fourteen-carat rule," officially noti-
fied in November 1966, the goldsmiths and *sarafs* achieved their immediate and primary objective. The Swarnakar Sangh was created
to fight the rules and, as of January 1967, it had no other program,
educational, social, or political, which might hold it together; its
president was unsure of its future. There are other provisions of the
rules which are still in effect and to which the sangh still objects,
and the reorganization of the gold trade into *swarna-silpa* has never
even been seriously considered by the government. But with the
end of "quality control," the sangh lapsed into quiescence. There
have been no more protest meetings or processions. The sangh considered putting up B. A. Soni as a candidate in opposition to Morarji Desai in the 1967 general elections, but didn't. Manilal Rugnath
Rampara ran as a Jana Sangh candidate for the Gujarat Legislative
Assembly and was badly defeated. In no account of the general
elections that I have seen has what remains of gold control been
mentioned as an issue.

Sarafs may still not lend money and sell jewelry from the same
premises, and the same amendments to the rules which freed them
of the "fourteen-carat rule" put further legal restrictions on their
right to lend money on the mortgage of gold. They continue to object to these restrictions. But their customers have other things to
mortgage, and there is nothing new in the rules that is any more
difficult to evade than what has been in them all along. The "fourteen-carat rule" draped a pall of fear over the gold trade and its
customers; but when that pall was removed goldsmiths and *sarafs*
returned, more or less, to business as usual.

Bengal] Swarna Silpa Samiti, Rajasthan Sona Chandi Shrimik Sangh, Andhra
Pradesh Swarnakar Sangham, Delhi Goldsmith Workers Union.

124. *Lok Sabha Debates*, 23 August 1966, mimeographed.

125. Chaudhuri's statement was immediately challenged by a Congress
M.P., Kamalnayan Bajaj, who acknowledged that although there are regional
and traditional differences among goldsmith groups, "as far as the scrapping
of gold control is concerned, I think that there may not be any difference
among the deputations of *swarnakars* who have met the Finance Minister";
Ibid.

4　OPPOSITION PARTIES

The analogically inclined may find an element not unlike symbiosis in the relationships between interest groups and opposition parties in this study. The similarity is particularly striking, at least at first glance, in the case of the linguistic-provincial coalitions, where the mutually beneficial relationships between groups and party alliances were both internal and intimate. Like a lichen, the Samyukta Maharashtra Samiti was a single growth made up of elements living together in a mutually beneficial relationship. The interest groups supplied the party coalition with an issue and a constituency. The party coalition provided the interest groups with political skills, access to political arenas, and assistance from external sources; for example, the Communist party of India.

The analogy breaks down rapidly, however. It was in the linguistic-provincial coalitions, where the relationships between "symbionts" were most intimate, that they were subject to the greatest strain. The cohesion of groups was strained by the competition of political parties, and the relationships of local party units with parent and sibling units were disturbed by their involvement with interest groups. The Akhil Bharatiya Swarnakar Sangh, on the other hand, tied to no party or parties, was free to solicit the assistance of all and, insofar as that assistance was forthcoming, it was untouched by party rivalry. The opposition parties, in turn, were able to pursue their rivalries unrestrained by any institutional commitment to the goldsmiths while they derived whatever profits they could from being the *swarnakars'* champions.

During the period covered in this study and to the present, opposition parties in India have been largely incapable at the national level of aggregating oppositional inputs into alternative policies. That function has been Congress's. But the opposition parties in the cases here did perform a function which might be called penultimate aggregation: publicizing the issues and putting them in order

73

of political priority, bringing them into political arenas, and setting the political stakes – in a sense, wrapping up the oppositional package and delivering it. For example, the Samyukta Maharashtra Samiti and the Mahagujarat Janata Parishad, acting and threatening to act jointly during 1957 through 1959, presented Congress with guidelines for linguistic reorganization and an estimate of the price it would have to pay for not reorganizing. In the controversy over the Gold Control Rules, the opposition's unanimous disapproval of the rules, coupled with its relative freedom from involvements with associations in the gold trade, helped it cut through the tangled relationships between *swarnakars* and *sarafs* in which the issue might have become entangled. It focused attention relentlessly on the most obvious and apparent shortcomings of the rules, and confronted the government with an almost unanimous demand for a simple return to the status quo ante.

Linguism and Leftism

In Maharashtra and Gujarat, Andhra, Mysore, Kerala, Punjab, and wherever there has been a disputed district or *taluk*, linguistic-provincial movements have attracted opposition parties in India as honey attracts flies.[1] For the weak and poorly organized opposition parties, the disunited and fragmented opposition parties, the opposition parties rooted in particular communities and particular discontents, popular demands for linguistic reorganization have come as boons. They have provided issues on which they could unite in spite of ideological differences, constituencies ready-made to agitate and vote against the ruling party, and relatively small and manageable arenas.

In the middle 1950s, however, only in Maharashtra, of all the areas in western India, had parties in opposition to Congress taken root. Accounting for this growth is beyond our scope, but we might point out some of the streams that have nurtured it: under the leadership of Bal Gangadhar Tilak, mass and militant politicization occurred relatively early in Maharashtra, in the nationalist movement of the first two decades in the twentieth century. The Satyashodhak

1. Parts of this section first appeared in Robert W. Stern, "Maharashtrian Linguistic Provincialism and Indian Nationalism," *Pacific Affairs*, vol. 37, Spring 1964.

Samaj challenged Brahman domination in Maharashtra, including their domination of Tilak's Congress, and has constantly contributed to the growth of opposition parties. The Independent Labor party, later the Scheduled Castes Federation, appeared in the thirties and forties to challenge Congress as a spokesman for the untouchables. Non-Congress, and particularly Communist, unions have challenged Congress's position in the labor movement in Bombay city since the 1920s. The linguistic-provincial movement, a decade old when the States Reorganization Commission submitted its report, brought opposition groups together and gave their activities some focus. Finally, all these challenges to Congress's hegemony in Maharashtra have been directed by some of the most popular and skillful politicians that India has produced.

The opposition parties which came together into the Samyukta Maharashtra Samiti tapped all these streams, and put together an effective challenge to Congress dominance. In Gujarat and Nag-Vidarbha, opposition parties were so weak that their combined strength was still negligible. More than the movement for Samyukta Maharashtra, the movements for Mahagujarat and Mahavidarbha were reliant on dissident and dissenting-but-loyal Congressmen and nonparty groups as such. Not surprisingly, the Samyukta Maharashtra Samiti was organized as a coalition in which the constituent parties retained their own identities, had their own leaders in the Bombay Legislative Assembly, and even fought the 1957 general elections under their own banners, whereas, at least theoretically, the Janata Parishad and the Nag-Vidarbha Samiti were supraparty, unitary organizations.

As a party coalition the Samyukta Maharashtra Samiti was a leftist alliance led by the Communists and the Praja Socialists. The Congress Jana Parishad, after it left the Bombay PCC, became the samiti's third major constituent. But although the Jana Parishad was in the samiti, it was of the Congress, and it is best dealt with in the next chapter. The Republican party of India (RPI) and the Peasants and Workers party (PWP), both of which subscribe to "socialist" goals, the latter describing itself as "Marxist," were officially in the circle of the samiti's major parties. But, in fact, they played a secondary role to the PSP and the Communists, and were major only in comparison to such splinter leftist groups as the Kisan Mazdoor, Lal Nishan, and Revolutionary Communist parties. The two nonleftist parties in the samiti — the Jana Sangh, which, in effect, left the coalition in 1958, and the Hindu Sabha — counted for little.

The RPI was divided not only between Maharashtra and Mahavidarbha. Within the samiti it was split into rival factions: one under B. C. Kamble took its lead from the Praja Socialists and left the samiti in 1960 when the PSP did; another following the Communists remained in the samiti after bifurcation; and a faction of this faction under R. D. Bhandare eventually joined the Congress. The PWP, now the second party in Maharashtra, was little more than a rump of the Satyashodhak movement when its leaders Keshavrao Jedhe and S. S. More returned to Congress between the first and second general elections.[2]

For the Praja Socialists, leadership of the samiti presented an opportunity embedded in two problems. The opportunity, of course, was to become a major factor in Maharashtrian politics. The first problem was a matter of internal discipline. Could the PSP, as a national party, work out a linguistic-provincial reorganization policy for western India, convince or compel its units in Maharashtra, Gujarat, and Nag-Vidarbha to accept it, and survive the experience? The second problem, related to the first, was the Communists. If the PSP was going to lead the samiti it had no choice other than to do it in cooperation with the Communists. S. M. Joshi, the PSP leader in Maharashtra, advocated such cooperation; yet the prevailing sentiment among the party's national leaders, and to a lesser extent among Praja Socialists in Maharashtra, was anti-Communist. The Communists in Maharashtra, numerically weaker than the PSP but better disciplined, had more to gain and perhaps less to lose from such an alliance. Could the PSP ride the Communist tiger without winding up inside it?

The Maharashtrian Praja Socialists seized the opportunity and left the problems to their party to deal with as well as it could,

2. The Lal Nishan (Red Flag) party is an interesting offshoot of the non-Brahman movement in Maharashtra. It is, in effect, a local auxiliary of the Communist party with non-Brahman leadership. But like the PWP it has not remained exclusively non-Brahman. S. K. Limaye, a Brahman, is a major figure in the Lal Nishan. The PWP derives some strength in Marathwada from anti-Christian and anti-Muslim, rather than anti-Brahman, sentiments, according to Lalji Pendse, the leading chronicler of the Samyukta Maharashtra movement; interview, Bombay, 27 April 1967. In the 1967 general elections the PWP supported the candidacy of at least one Brahman, D. K. Kunte, a former Congressman and speaker of the Bombay Legislative Assembly.

which was not very well at all. In February 1956, a month after the Maharashtra PCC left the Samyukta Maharashtra Parishad, S. M. Joshi, in cooperation with the Communists, took the lead in organizing the samiti and committing it to an uncompromising struggle for Samyukta Maharashtra. But not six months later the leading Praja Socialists in Parliament, Ashok Mehta and Acharya J. B. Kripalani, advocated the creation of "big bilingual" Bombay.[3] Thus, while Ashok Mehta, in New Delhi, was calling for an end to the samiti's agitation, S. M. Joshi in Bombay was calling for its "intensification." [4] The PSP was simply unable to handle the issue of linguistic-provincial reorganization in western India as a unified, national party.

In Gujarat, Praja Socialists played a leading role in founding the Mahagujarat Janata Parishad and in bringing Indulal Yajnik to its leadership. Their collaborators in organizing Gujarati linguistic-provincialism were the Communists. Thus they found themselves in ambiguous relationships of cooperation-competition with Communist colleagues in the Janata Parishad whom they distrusted and feared, and with Praja Socialist colleagues in the Samyukta Maharashtra Samiti whom they confronted in a linguistic-provincial controversy. At the PSP's fourth national conference in 1958, members from Gujarat expressed serious reservations about the party's growing entanglements with the Communists, and at the same time tried to get its support for the parishad's claims to disputed border areas between Maharashtra and Gujarat.[5] By 1958, the national PSP officially supported the creation of Samyukta Maharashtra and Mahagujarat, but it was never able to arbitrate a bifurcation settlement between its units in Maharashtra and Gujarat.[6]

Sureshchandra Gangrede, a Praja Socialist, was one of the founders of the Nag-Vidarbha Andolan Samiti, and other Praja Socialists were either prominent in it or, like Acharya Kripalani, prominent in support of Mahavidarbha.[7] So prominent that in November 1959 the PSP's resolution welcoming the impending creation of Maharashtra was amended to specify "including [Nag-]Vidarbha." The mover of the amendment explained: "Some leaders of the party are

3. *Lok Sabha Debates*, vol. 6, part 2, 26 July–9 August 1956.

4. *Hindu*, 3 August 1956, and *Statesman*, 2 August 1956.

5. Praja Socialist Party, *Report of the Fourth National Conference* (Poona, 25–28 May 1958).

6. Ibid., and Praja Socialist Party, *Report of the Fifth National Conference* (Bombay, 5–9 November 1959).

7. *Hindustan Standard*, 26 September 1959.

saying that the party supports the demand for a separate [Nag-] Vidarbha. This creates confusion amongst the workers of the party." [8]

An alternative to Mahavidarbha, although not one seriously considered by anyone with power to decide, was "Chhattisgarh-Vidarbha," a new bilingual state to be composed of Nag-Vidarbha and
the largely tribal, mineral-rich Chhattisgarh region of Madhya Pradesh. Although this scheme was opposed by the Nag-Vidarbha
Samiti and its Praja Socialist members, its most vigorous proponents
were Khubchand Baghel and Brijlal Verma, PSP members of the
Madhya Pradesh Legislative Assembly.[9] Baghel's and Verma's
sponsorship of "Chhattisgarh-Vidarbha" was dismissed by the PSP
chairman in Madhya Pradesh as their "individual opinion" which
did not reflect the party's position,[10] although it apparently did reflect the position of V. Y. Tamaskar, the PSP leader in the legislative
assembly.[11]

Finally, in November 1958, when Praja Socialists from Maharashtra joined their samiti colleagues in a *hartal* in Belgaum and Karwar
towns to protest their noninclusion in Samyukta Maharashtra, they
did so over the protest of Praja Socialists from Mysore.[12]

Fears of what might come from collaboration with the Communists
haunted the PSP. At its conference at Bangalore in November 1956,
the party resolved to have "no alliance, entanglement, or adjustment
[in the 1957 general elections] with Congress, communalists, or the
Communists." [13] But under pressure from S. M. Joshi, whom one
leftist journal called the "Indian Nenni," [14] and the Maharashtra
PSP, which had in fact become allied and entangled with the Communists in February, the party's national executive bowed to
"necessity." [15] "Abject surrender," said a leading Gujarati Praja
Socialist.[16] Prem Bhasin, the party's joint secretary, speaking at its
1958 conference in Poona, raised no objection to this characteriza-

8. Praja Socialist Party, *Report of the Fifth National Conference.*
9. *Hitavada,* 28 June 1959.
10. H. V. Kamath in ibid., 22 July 1959.
11. Ibid., 19 September 1959.
12. *Free Press Journal,* 2 November 1958.
13. Praja Socialist Party, *Report of the Third National Conference* (Bangalore, 25–28 November 1956; New Delhi, 1956).
14. *Link,* 8 November 1959, p. 10.
15. S. M. Joshi, interview, New Delhi, 1 April 1967.
16. Amul Desai, in Praja Socialist Party, *Report of the Fourth National Conference.*

tion: "If it can be termed a surrender, well yes, the National Executive did surrender." And if they had not surrendered? "I am sure," the battle-wise veteran of the Indian socialist movement concluded, "there would have been no Poona conference in that case." [17] Even so, opposition within the party, particularly from Gujarat, to the Maharashtra PSP's alliance with the Communists continued, and it was by no means absent from the Maharashtra PSP itself. Particularly in the Bombay Municipal Corporation, where the party was led by the anti-Communist Moinuddin Harris, Praja Socialists fought with the Communists constantly. And efforts by either samiti or PSP leaders to limit these battles were generally unavailing. In many cases the battles had nothing to do with Samyukta Maharashtra.

To the embarrassment of the Communists, Praja Socialists in the Bombay Corporation supported a Congress-sponsored resolution condemning the execution of the former Hungarian prime minister and rebel leader, Imre Nagy.[18] A group of Praja Socialists, defying not only the samiti but their own leaders, threatened to resign from the corporation and thus turn it back to Congress control unless they were granted a "free vote" to congratulate the Nehru government for dismissing the Communist ministry in Kerala.[19] In 1959, China's suppression of rebellion in Tibet and its occupation of territory in Ladakh and the Northeast Frontier Agency precipitated a crisis in the samiti. The Praja Socialists in the Bombay Corporation led the attack. In May they sponsored a motion to send a corporation-supported medical mission to Tibet,[20] and in September, after India's dispute with China had advanced beyond the state of policy disagreement over Tibet to a heated controversy over Chinese occupation of the Aksai Chin plateau in Ladakh and territory south of the McMahon Line on the northeast frontier, the Praja Socialists in the Bombay Corporation introduced a motion to condemn Chinese "aggression." [21]

Praja Socialists fought with the Communists over the means and

17. Ibid.
18. *Free Press Journal,* 12 July 1958.
19. *Times of India,* 21 August 1959. The Kerala PSP, it might be added, was among the most active participants in the "liberation struggle" which led to the immobilization of the Communist ministry and its dismissal under Article 356 of the Indian constitution, the provision for the establishment of "President's Rule."
20. Ibid., 14 May 1959.
21. Ibid., 20 September 1959.

ends of the samiti. Frequently the Praja Socialists, and not only to
the annoyance of the Communists, acted as a brake on the samiti's
tactics and ambitions. The PSP cooperated with the Communists in
the "general strike" in Bombay city in November 1956, but refused
to lend its support to another one in January 1957. In 1959, S. M.
Joshi threatened to resign as general secretary rather than participate in a Communist-planned *hartal* in Bombay city to protest the
Congress Working Committee's award of border areas to Gujarat
and Mysore.[22] According to the Communist leader and samiti president, S. A. Dange, Joshi was "worried," unnecessarily, about
violence.[23]

Although S. M. Joshi rejected the possibility of forming a samiti
coalition government for Maharashtra which would include the "an-
tinational" Communists, unlike many of his PSP colleagues, he was
not averse to prolonging the samiti's life beyond bifurcation. But
there was little enthusiasm among Praja Socialists for this. In May
1960, the month of bifurcation, six months after Joshi had made his
"irrevocable decision" to resign, the PSP left the samiti. The Congress Jana Parishad had already returned to the Congress fold in
December 1959. With the PSP's departure, the samiti was reduced
to a leftist rump, shorn of two of its three principal constituents. But
for the PSP this was scant consolation. It left the samiti for the wil-
derness. Only a faction of the RPI followed it out. As one observer
noted, "Whether it is Imre Nagy, Tibet, Kerala, or any such extra-
neous issue, the Samiti has been divided, not between the Communists and the rest, but between the PSP and most of the other
groups." [24]

In Gujarat, no less than in Maharashtra, the PSP was unable to
cope successfully with its two problems of internal discipline and
Communist alliance, and this failure cost it whatever opportunity it
might have had to ride the issue of linguistic-provincialism to a
prominent place in the politics of western India. It took upon itself
the burden of leadership and then it failed to lead. The supraparty
Mahagujarat Janata Parishad was formed largely through the initiative of PSP leaders, but they were unwilling to run their candidates
under the parishad's banner in southern Gujarat or Saurashtra and

22. Ibid., 22 November 1959, and *Free Press Journal*, 25 December 1959.
The *hartal* was cancelled and Joshi postponed his resignation.
23. Interview, New Delhi, 21 June 1967.
24. *Times of India*, 15 October 1959.

unable to arrive at an amicable division with the Communists of some constituencies in Ahmadabad city's industrial areas. Praja Socialists supported Indulal Yajnik for president of the parishad and then regretted it because he seemed to be closer to the Communists. In Saurashtra, some of them continued to support the "three-unit" formula, whereas in Gujarat proper they did not.

Outside Bombay city, the Communist party had been able to make little headway in western India, even less than the PSP.[25] The Samyukta Maharashtra Samiti and the Mahagujarat Janata Parishad were its opportunities to take the lead on the popular issue of linguistic-provincialism and to do so as the dominant member in blocs of smaller or less well disciplined parties. Certainly it would not be able to control the samiti and Janata Parishad as completely as it had controlled the Andhra Mahasabha. And the democratic socialists and bourgeois democrats in Maharashtra and Gujarat were unlikely to rally to an insurrectionary "Telengana movement." [26] But this would be unnecessary. In 1956, at the twentieth congress of the CPSU, the "parliamentary road to power" had officially been opened for the Indian Communists by none other than Chairman Khrushchev. Nothing in the CPI's recent experience of violent uprisings and successful suppressions suggested that it would have much to lose by following it. It contested about one and a half times the percentage of seats in the second general elections as it had in the first, and came out of them the second party in India (albeit a poor second), and the first in Kerala, where it formed the first Communist government to be brought to power through democratic elections. In 1958 at Amritsar the CPI formulated a "thesis" which committed it to seek power primarily through the electoral-parliamentary systems as the leader of "left unity" blocs. The samiti and the Janata Parishad had proved themselves to be excellent opportunities. The Communists rose from relative obscurity to leadership of

25. In the first general elections, the two parties which were later to form the PSP won 9 seats in the Bombay Legislative Assembly and 17 percent of the votes polled. In contrast the Communists won 1 seat and less than 2 percent of the popular vote. The KMPP and Socialist parties contested a total of 249 seats and the Communists contested 24.

26. One of the major events leading up to the creation of a Telegu-language Andhra Pradesh was serious agrarian uprisings between 1948 and 1950 in the Telengana region of Hyderabad, led by the Communist-dominated Andhra Mahasabha. In some places peasant soviets were established, but the movement was finally suppressed by the government.

the opposition because of their participation in them. Unlike the
Praja Socialists, but for the same reason, the Communists became
the champions of preserving the coalitions even after Maharashtra
and Gujarat states had been created.

This is not to say that their involvement in the samiti and the Janata Parishad posed no problems for the Communists. But at least at
the tactical level the Communists were more successful than the
Praja Socialists in adjusting themselves to operating in alliance with
other parties. A. K. Gopalan, the Communist leader in the Lok
Sabha, characterized "big bilingual" Bombay as "a new conspiracy
against the Maharashtrians" [27] and the Communist M.P.s voted en
bloc against it. Contrast this to the situation in the PSP, where leaders in Delhi were saying and doing one thing while leaders in western and central India were saying and doing a variety of other
things!

The CPI rejected both Mahavidarbha and Chhattisgarh-Vidarbha, and was better able than the PSP to establish a common bifurcation formula for its people in Maharashtra and Gujarat. But the
effects of its participation in linguistic-provincial politics on the
CPI's internal cohesion were, if anything, more profound. The extension of "polycentrism" to the Indian Communist movement, and
the fragmentation of that movement into a "nationalist" Communist
party and a militant "pro-Peking" party, were outgrowths of the co-
incidence of the CPI's leadership of the linguistic-provincial movement in western India and the Sino-Indian border conflict which
began in 1959.

The PSP's badgering forced the issue. At first the Maharashtrian
Communists, like the CPI, were disdainful of the Tibetan "counter-
revolutionaries," and following the Soviet lead, took no sides and
assessed no blame in the border controversy. They tried to detoxify
the issue of Sino-Indian relations in the samiti by sponsoring a motion to declare it and other such issues beyond the range of the samiti's concern,[28] and they attempted to isolate the Praja Socialists in
the samiti by discrediting them as wreckers and turncoats.[29] A
cause célèbre in the samiti was the Communist attack on S. M. Joshi
for his "unauthorized" meeting with Nehru in November 1959, a

---

27. *Times of India,* 5 August 1956.
28. *New Age,* 12 July 1959.
29. See the debates in the Bombay Municipal Corporation, *Times of India,*
22, 26, 30 September and 10 October 1959.

meeting at which, it was implied, the possibility of Congress-Praja Socialist cooperation in postbifurcation Maharashtra was discussed.[30]

It didn't work. The Kamble faction of the RPI was growing increasingly critical of the CPI's position on the border controversy. And more important, the Maratha Peasants and Workers party, which had generally sided with the CPI in its battles with the Praja Socialists and had come out of the 1957 elections as the leading opposition party in Maharashtra, condemned the "aggressive activities" of China and censured the CPI for not taking a "nationalistic" stand on the issue.[31] Two months later, S. M. Joshi broke his "self-imposed ordinance" not to speak from a partisan platform and roundly condemned the CPI for its position on Sino-Indian relations. The samiti alliance, he said, could not be preserved as a nationalist opposition group after the creation of Maharashtra if the Communists continued as members of it.[32] In spite of his difficulties with the Communists and theirs with him, S. M. Joshi was the one link between the increasingly restive PSP and the samiti, and the Communists' one hope for preserving the alliance beyond the day of bifurcation. Now, under the shadow of Chinese "aggression" and the CPI's failure to label it as such, that hope was fading.

The Maharashtrian Communists were confronted with a choice between "proletarian internationalism," which had never paid off for the CPI,[33] and linguistic-provincialism, which had. They chose the latter. Less than a week after Dange's unsuccessful attempt to get the CPI's central executive committee to make a general statement in support of the Government of India's border position, the samiti's parliamentary board, with its Communist members in attendance and Dange presiding, resolved that the "provocative attitude of China had violated the basic spirit" of Sino-Indian friendship, that the presence of Chinese soldiers in Ladakh and the Northeast Frontier Agency was "tantamount to forcible occupation," and that the McMahon Line was India's "natural boundary in the northeast."[34] S. G. Sardesai, the secretary of the Maharashtra CP,

30. Joshi denies this, and these charges were the immediate cause of his "irrevocable decision" to resign as samiti general secretary.

31. *Times of India*, 29 September 1959.

32. *Janata*, 11 October 1959.

33. The CPI's experiences with its "international environment" are documented in Gene D. Overstreet and Marshall Windmiller, *Communism in India* (Berkeley: University of California Press, 1960).

34. *Times of India*, 8 October 1959.

told the central executive committee of the CPI at its meeting in
October 1959 that the Communists could not have remained in the
Samyukta Maharashtra Samiti had they not gone along with their
allies' condemnation of the Chinese.[35] Dange went a step further
when the Chinese destroyed an Indian patrol in Ladakh, to that
date the most dramatic incident in the conflict. He explicitly
blamed the incident on the Chinese.[36] Like the Maharashtrian
Communists, the Communists in the Mahagujarat Janata Parishad
were compelled by their allies to rally to the support of the Indian
government.[37]

The attempts by Maharashtrian and Gujarati Communists to preserve the linguistic-provincial coalitions in western India by con-
forming to the nationalist sentiments of their allies were unsuccessful. But they changed the face of Communism in India. At Meerut
in November 1959 the party's national council, after censuring the
Maharashtrian rebels for indiscipline, appointed their leader,
Dange, to a policy-reviewing triumverate, praised their work, and,
for the most part, accepted their position on Sino-Indian relations as
its own.[38] In 1962 Dange, his reputation as a leader of popular
fronts enhanced by his leadership of the samiti and his successful
fight against the party's "internationalists," was elected to the new
post of CPI chairman. In the Sino-Indian war of that year the party,
in spite of warnings against "chauvinism" from *Pravda* and rum-
blings of discontent among its leftist militants, stated unequivocally
its support for the war efforts of the Indian government. In 1964,
the militants broke away and formed the Communist party of In-
dia-Marxist, the Left Communist party. And although contemp-
tuous of the "Dange clique" the Left Communists have by and large
followed its lead down the parliamentary path as leaders, with it or
against it, of "left unity" blocs.

Political and ideological discord among their constituent units in-
hibited the development of the Samyukta Maharashtra Samiti and
the Mahagujarat Janata Parishad into anything beyond single-issue
opposition fronts, and on several occasions it threatened to pull

35. Ibid., 7 November 1959.
36. *Statesman*, 25 October 1959. The CPI secretariat merely noted that the
official Indian and Chinese descriptions of the incident differed, assessed no
blame, and counseled caution: *New Age*, 1 November 1959.
37. *Times of India*, 16 November 1959.
38. *New Age*, 22 November 1959.

them apart. Yet they were able to hold together for three crucial years. In those years, separately and together, they were able to mobilize the sentiments for linguistic-provincial reorganization in their areas into three major inputs to the Congress "system."

First, they threatened immediately Congress's dominant position in the parliamentary system of Maharashtra and they posed a possible future threat to its dominance in Gujarat. Second, they confronted the Congress government of Bombay with massive "direct action" campaigns which it could not conciliate, could not suppress, and could not manage without increasing the intensity of opposition by raising the level of violence. Finally, they presented Congress with an outline of a plan for reorganization. For the remainder of this chapter these inputs will be discussed.

The allocation of electoral constituencies among the component groups in the Samyukta Maharashtra Samiti and the Mahagujarat Janata Parishad in preparation for the 1957 general elections was a process attended with controversy. In some cases the controversy continued into the election campaign. A. B. Kulkarni reports that in Sholapur district, the one area in Maharashtra in which Congress retained its strength, the allocation of legislative assembly constituencies "created bitter feelings among the component parties and certain parties, for instance Jana Sangh, refrained from participating in the electioneering activities of the samiti." [39] In some cases samiti candidates competed not only with Congressmen but with samiti dissidents. [40] In Gujarat, the PSP insisted on running candidates under its own banners in southern Gujarat and Saurashtra. [41] In spite of their difficulties, however, the coalitions used the polls to advantage.

In Maharashtra and Bombay city, Congress was badly defeated by the samiti in 1957. In the 1952 general elections Congress had won 139 of 170 seats in the Bombay Legislative Assembly from Maharashtra and Bombay city and 19 of 22 seats in the Lok Sabha. It came out of the 1957 general elections with only 33 of 136 seats in the legislative assembly from Maharashtra and 2 of the 22 seats in

39. A. B. Kulkarni, *The Second General Elections in Sholapur* (Sholapur: Institute of Public Administration, 1957).
40. *Hitavada*, 23 February 1957.
41. D. N. Pathak et al., *Three General Elections in Gujarat* (Ahmadabad: Gujarat University, 1966).

the Lok Sabha. It lost the Bombay city Municipal Corporation and half of the city's legislative assembly and Lok Sabha seats. The only Marathi-speaking areas of "big bilingual" Bombay which sent a Congress majority to the legislative assembly and Parliament were Nag-Vidarbha and Marathwada, where the samiti was not active.[42] Some Congress politicians attempted to minimize the party's humiliation. The Union home minister, for example, noted that a "majority of members" returned to the Lok Sabha from Bombay state supported the bilingual arrangement, that is, were disciplined Congressmen. But the message had been delivered and its contents were clear. Sadiq Ali, the Congress general secretary, summed it up. The elections in Maharashtra, he wrote, were "an ocular demonstration of the fact that when the mass mind is roused nothing avails against it." [43]

Contrary to the expectations, or at least the hopes, of some Congress leaders, the issue of Samyukta Maharashtra, like the samiti, would not fade from the polls. Of the twelve legislative assembly and parliamentary by-elections held in the Marathi-speaking areas of Bombay state between 1957 and 1960, Congress won only three. Two, for the Lok Sabha seat from Baramati (Poona district) and the assembly seat from Mangrulpir (Akola district in Vidarbha), were contested in February 1960 *after* the Congress-Government elite had announced its decision to bifurcate the state. The third, the Nagpur Lok Sabha seat, was won by M. S. Aney, and, as he pointed out to the chief minister, his was a victory for Mahavidarbha and not for the perpetuation of the bilingual state.[44]

Only after the general elections did the samiti make an effort to cultivate Marathwada and Nag-Vidarbha. It supported a resolution for one annual meeting of the legislative assembly in Nagpur city, a provision of the Nagpur Pact which the chief minister had said could not be put into effect in bilingual Bombay.[45] At rallies in Nag-Vidarbha, R. D. Bhandare, of the RPI, and P. K. Atre tried to woo the scheduled castes away from the Nag-Vidarbha Andolan

42. In Nag-Vidarbha, Congress won all eleven Lok Sabha seats and fifty-five of the sixty-three seats in the Legislative Assembly. In Marathwada, Congress won six of the seven Lok Sabha seats and thirty-five of the forty-two assembly seats.

43. All-India Congress Committee, *The General Elections of 1957: A Survey* (New Delhi, 1959).

44. *Hitavada*, 12 January 1959.

45. *Statesman*, 27 August 1957.

Samiti.[46] In 1959, when the AICC met in Nagpur city the Samyukta Maharashtra Samiti held a rival meeting.[47] It contested the district level board elections in Marathwada in 1958, and beat Congress in three out of five districts.[48] Of the nine by-elections lost by Congress, three were in Marathwada and one in Nag-Vidarbha (Amravati), where a former Congress MLA with samiti support defeated Congress and Nag-Vidarbha samiti rivals. Thus, in the only Marathi-speaking districts spared to Congress in the general elections the tide seemed to be turning.

In Bombay city, the future for Congress appeared ominous. Two of the legislative assembly by-elections it lost were in the city. One seat was retained by the samiti and one gained. It was becoming increasingly clear that the Bombay PCC's opposition to turning the city over to the Marhattas was leading, ironically, to its capture by the samiti. And the samiti in Bombay city, perpetually on the brink of dissolution, wouldn't dissolve. The PSP spurned Bombay PCC President K. K. Shah's "sporting" offer to abandon the Communists and collaborate with the Congress in managing the corporation.[49] It would support Congress's position in Kerala, Tibet, and Ladakh, but not in Bombay city. Indulal Yajnik reported that in March or April 1959, S. K. Patil, the principal figure in the Bombay Congress, told him that there was no point in continuing the bilingual arrangement.[50] Patil, according to Deogirikar, "had gradually come round."[51]

The remaining three by-elections lost by the Congress were in Maharashtra for seats which were retained by the samiti, two with increased margins.

In Gujarat, the situation faced by Congress after the elections was anomalous but portentous. The leftist leaders of the Mahagujarat Janata Parishad were opening a breach on the right. Congress's losses to the parishad and the PSP, although serious enough, were hardly staggering. Only in Ahmadabad city and the surrounding districts of Ahmadabad, Kaira, and Mehsana were they significant. In Ahmadabad city the municipal corporation was taken over

46. *Bombay Chronicle*, 30 August 1958, and *Hitavada*, 29 August 1959.
47. *Express*, 11 January 1959.
48. *Free Press Journal*, 8 May 1958.
49. Ibid., 3 August 1959.
50. Interview.
51. T. R. Deogirikar, *Twelve Years in Parliament: Democracy in Action* (Poona: Chitrashala Prakashan, 1964), p. 297.

by the dissident Congressmen of the Nagarik Paksh. In Ahmadabad district Congress lost nine of the fourteen legislative assembly seats, in Kaira it lost eight of thirteen, and in Mehsana eleven of twelve. Of the remaining fifty-two legislative assembly seats from Gujarat, however, Congress won forty-five. Congress lost five of the fifteen Lok Sabha seats from Gujarat, all from Ahmadabad, Kaira, and Mehsana districts. All the non-Congress candidates elected to the legislative assembly or the Lok Sabha were affiliated with the parishad. In the rest of Gujarat, Congress held its own, and in Saurashtra and Kutch it swept the field.[52]

After the elections, the badly divided parishad rapidly lost its grip. Its membership declined precipitously between 1956 and 1958, from about 182,000 to 37,000, and "direct action" campaigns, although momentarily stimulating, would not reverse the trend.[53] It lost all five of the by-elections held in the years after the second general elections. One of these was in Kaira and another in Ahmadabad.

But, although the leftist-led linguistic-provincial movement was fading, in part because it was leftist led and in part because it lacked the emotional intensity and mass base which it had in Maharashtra, it was reawakening and remobilizing the anti–land reform peasant parties, the Khedut Sangh, which had been lying dormant since their defeat in 1952. The Mahagujarat Janata Parishad served as a bridge in time between the Khedut Sangh and the Swatantra party of Gujarat, which was founded in the Kaira district town of Nadiad in 1960. It was not the only bridge, but particularly in Mehsana and Kaira districts, and to a lesser extent in Ahmadabad, where there is some leftist strength in the city, it was a major span.

Mehsana and Kaira were two of the three districts in Gujarat proper (not including Kutch) in which the Swatantra party did best in the 1962 general elections. In the first general elections in 1952 the Lok Paksha (People's party), which was affiliated with the Khedut Sangh, won its highest percentage of the popular vote in Kaira, and the highest percentage of the vote won by independent "rightist candidates" was in Mehsana.[54] In Ahmadabad the Krishikar

52. Of forty-one assembly seats from Saurashtra and Kutch, Congress lost one.
53. Government of Bombay, *Report of the Commission of Inquiry.*
54. Pathak, *Three General Elections,* p. 45.

Lok Paksha, also an affiliate of the Khedut Sangh, and rightist candidates were active.

Professor N. G. Ranga, president of the conservative All-India Agriculturalists' Federation and later president of the Swatantra party, had close ties to the Khedut Sangh. His election as president of the Swatantra party, the announcement of its founding first at a meeting of the Agriculturalists' Federation, and party leaders' references to the Congress's Nagpur resolution on cooperative joint farming as the last straw were meant to symbolize Swatantra's ties to the (landed) peasantry.[55]

Bhailalbhai D. Patel, the present leader of the Swatantra party in Gujarat, was one of the founders of the Mahagujarat Parishad at Vallabh Vidyanagar in Kaira district, and he was a leading light of the Lok Paksha. A well-known Gandhian "constructive worker" and an active rural modernizer, Bhailalbhai was a "major entrant" into the new party.[56] Dadubhai Amin of Ahmadabad was one of the founders of the Krishikar Lok Paksha, a leader of the Janata Parishad in 1957, and a Swatantra candidate for the legislative assembly in 1962. Purshottamdas Patel and his followers from Mehsana first left the Congress in protest against the Bombay Tenancy Act of 1948, returned, and left again to join the Janata Parishad, for which they won its most spectacular victory, all the legislative assembly seats from Mehsana but one. In 1960 Purshottamdas returned to Congress again, but "the Swatantra party was largely formed out of a powerful section of the Purshottamdas group that refused to join the Congress."[57] When the parishad disbanded, the Swatantra party, which had not existed when it was formed, could claim about 20 percent of its delegation to the legislative assembly. The *Hindu* speculated that along with the fear of losing Maharashtra to the samiti, apprehension about the growth of the Swatantra party in Gujarat was "uppermost in the mind of the Prime Minister" when he decided to bifurcate.[58]

In sum, by 1960 the prospects in bilingual Bombay for Congress in the looming third general elections were not bright. K. K. Shah said at one point after the 1957 general elections that "Congressmen

---

55. Howard L. Erdman, *The Swatantra Party and Indian Conservativism* (Cambridge: Cambridge University Press, 1967), chap. 4.
56. Ibid., pp. 132-33.
57. Pathak, *Three General Elections*, p. 191.
58. 13 November 1959.

are prepared to lose the next elections and remain in the opposition . . . on this issue [of the preservation of bilingual Bombay]." [59] But, of course, they weren't.

Congress's sensitivity to threatening oppositional inputs to the electoral-parliamentary systems is self-evident. The systems are its creations. In four general elections held over a period of fifteen years, Congress has been their most successful manipulator; and insofar as India fits, or fit, the model of a "one-party dominant" system it has been largely because Congress dominated the polls and the legislatures. Leading Congressmen are generally quite candid about their interest in winning elections. For example, U. N. Dhebar, who was the Congress president during most of the time covered in this study and is one of the key figures in it, does not hesitate to attribute the Congress-Government elite's decision to bifurcate Bombay to its fear of losing the 1962 elections in the state.[60]

But "direct action" is another matter. It is neither in Congress's ideological nor in its political interests to acknowledge the legitimacy or the efficacy of "direct action." Nehru's words to the June 1956 meeting of the AICC in Bombay, a city which had experienced nine months of intermittent and widespread violence growing out of "direct action" campaigns, are fairly typical:

This great organization, the Indian National Congress has faced thousands of difficulties. It has fought a mighty empire and has succeeded in liberating the country. Are we now to be cowed down by threats of violence and stone throwing and intimidation . . . ? It was foolish to imagine that acts of stone throwing would shake the Government. The Government is not so weak that such acts can force it to concede demands.[61]

Undoubtedly, it is not merely the "acts of stone throwing" which are significant oppositional inputs. But, to pursue the metaphor, the stones, like stones thrown into a pool, send out ripples which disturb the water's surface beyond where they have landed.

"Direct action," regardless of the intentions of its planners, frequently turns violent or threatens violence. The hooligan element which is a part of the population in almost every Indian city, the *goondas,* if no one else, almost insure that here will be violence.

59. *Free Press Journal,* 17 September 1958.
60. Interview, New Delhi, 12 April 1967.
61. Quoted in Deogirikar, *Twelve Years in Parliament,* p. 215.

Where Communists, or others who are not as "worried" about violence as S. M. Joshi was, lead strikes and demonstrations, the chances of violence, of course, increase.

Estimating from Bayley's figures for 1955 and 1958, about 20 to 25 percent of the time "direct action" is met with police firing.[62] Police firing in India, as elsewhere, has a tendency to intensify opposition and hostility. From all reports, this was true in Bombay city, where demonstrations and police firings accompanied almost every major setback for the Marhattas. In its report on the rioting in Ahmadabad in 1958, the Kotval Commission observed that immediately after the police firings of two years earlier, "the anti-Congress feeling was a general feeling amongst the people uninspired by any other persons or political parties." [63] Pathak et al. make the interesting observation that, aside from Ahmadabad, the Mahagujarat movement was strongest in those districts, Mehsana and Kaira, where, among other things of course, there had been police firings.[64]

Demands for judical inquries into police firings, as common as the firings themselves, send out their own ripples. The then president of the Maharashtra PCC explained why the Bombay government refused the demands for a judicial inquiry into the police firings in Bombay city in November 1956 and January 1957:

> Not that the Government would have lost anything; but during the process of inquiry wounds would have been reopened, bitterness would have increased, and passions would have flared up. It was for that fear that the inquiry was not granted.[65]

The refusal, however, did bring on the resignation of the Union finance minister, C. D. Deshmukh, a Marhatta and a highly respected "nonpolitical" financial expert. The resignation was itself a cause célèbre. And in explaining his reasons for resigning, Deshmukh drew a most embarrassing picture of the Government of India's decision-making processes at the highest level. The Kotval Commission, whose inquiry was sanctioned by the Government of Bombay, could not trace the order to fire on the students of Ahmadabad to the government. But it is difficult not to conclude from its

62. Quoted in Myron Weiner, *The Politics of Scarcity* (Chicago: University of Chicago Press, 1962), p. 207.
63. Government of Bombay, *Report of the Commission of Inquiry.*
64. In the towns of Kalol and Nadiad: Pathak, *Three General Elections*, p. 58.
65. Deogirikar, *Twelve Years in Parliament*, p. 209.

report that the chief minister behaved tactlessly and insensitively when the "three-unit" formula was aborted.

"Direct action" and violence reveal, as perhaps nothing else does, the clay feet on which the "dominant party" stands. The laws of its legislatures are flouted, its ministers and its candidates for public office are stoned, humiliated, and prohibited from appearing in public, its meetings are disturbed and forced to be cancelled, and its inability to maintain public order or to meet popular demands is made manifest.

Look at violence through Congress eyes! The then president of the Maharashtra PCC describes the meeting in 1956 of the AICC in Bombay city as follows:

> The members of the A. I. C. C. were spat upon, Gandhi caps were forcibly removed, they were jeered at, and all ugly scenes were enacted. Even Panditji's [Nehru's] speech which usually attracts huge crowds, had a poor attendance. . . . When the meeting was going on, rumbling sounds of shouting were heard from a distance and we were all the while fearing that the mob, if successful in breaking the police cordon, would . . . break the meeting.[66]

The election campaign in 1957 went no better:

> The present writer, as head of the Congress organization in Maharashtra, addressed several meetings for canvassing support to the Congress candidates. No meeting passed off peacefully. Stones were thrown, abusive language was used, anti-Congress slogans were raised, cars were smashed and meetings were broken. Nothing was safe not even the journey. Other Congress leaders were hesitating to face the people. Shri Chavan [the chief minister] bravely faced the ordeal. He was not met with better fate. Shri Jawarharlalji [Nehru], Pantji [the home minister], Dhebar, Morarji [Desai] addressed meetings for the election; but they were ineffective.[67]

And in Gujarat when the Congress-Government elite announced its acceptance of the "big bilingual" formula:

> The *hartals*, the processions, rowdyism, *lathi* [stave] charges [by the police], tear-gas, firings, desecrations, curfew orders, arson, riots, and lootings were all observable. . . . Derailment of trains was not left out. The *goonda* element got the upper hand. Resignations from Congress, from municipal and legislative bodies of Congressmen were in plenty. About fifteen persons were shot dead, hundreds were injured. There were about a thousand arrests. The workers in the textile mills struck work, students

66. Ibid., p. 214.
67. Ibid., p. 227.

boycotted the schools and colleges, the shop-keepers kept their shops shut. The whole civic life came to a stand-still. It was a miniature rebellion. Shri Morarji Desai went on a purificatory fast for eight days. . . . But the wrath of the people did not subside at least in Ahmadabad.[68]

By 1959 the risks of violence had, if anything, increased. The samiti and the parishad, which had been experimenting with sending representatives to each other's "direct action" campaigns,[69] threatened a massive joint campaign to begin in November. Their stated objective was either to compel the Congress-Government elite to bifurcate or, failing that, to topple the Bombay government. "The people," declared the parliamentary board of the samiti, "have the right to unseat a constitutionally elected government before its term by peaceful direct action in case it forfeits the confidence of the people." [70]

The Praja Socialists, who had acted as a restraining force on the samiti's "direct action" programs in the past, were in on the threat for November. The Communists, who by then were dominant in the samiti, were enraged at Congress's support for the movement to bring down their ministry in Kerala and were threatening revenge.[71] The non-Congress labor unions which had played a prominent part in the havoc in Bombay city were menacing. S. A. Dange and S. M. Joshi were using the linguistic-provincial agitation to resuscitate the Girni Kamgar Union in the textile industry. This posed a threat not only to the Congress-controlled INTUC in the industry, but, because the Communists frankly viewed the union as a political weapon, to Congress's already deteriorated position in the city.[72] In Ahmadabad, the Mahagujarat Janata Parishad, badly weakened by its split with the Nagarik Paksh, was counting more and more on "direct action" campaigns to restore its élan.

In August, a month after the joint agitation threat had first been made, the Congress-Government elite decided to reopen the Bombay reorganization issue. In October, a month before the joint agitation was to begin, Nehru acknowledged that the issue was being reexamined. In his announcement he stressed that the reexamination was taking place at a time when "everything was quiet and

68. Ibid., p. 225.
69. Samiti leaders, for example, were invited to participate and did participate in the parishad's demonstration in Ahmadabad in August 1958.
70. *Free Press Journal*, 6 July 1959.
71. Ibid., 4 August 1959.
72. *New Age*, 12 July 1959.

normal." [73] He must have known, however, that it was merely the quiet before the storm. And there was apparent unanimity in the belief that fear of the impending storm had played no small part in his decision.[74]

There are oppositional inputs which might be called, for lack of a better word, facilitative. These occur when opposition parties suggest alternatives to government policies, and the government, instead of defending itself against their suggestions, adopts them, not infrequently to the disadvantage of the parties which made the suggestions.

The "big bilingual" formula, although only partially successful, illustrates this class. It was supported in Parliament by anti-Communist Praja Socialist leaders who thought, or hoped, that in providing an alternative to "three-units" it would obviate a Praja Socialist-Communist alliance in Maharashtra. It doubtless appeared to be facilitative to the Congress-Government elite. They liked it more than the "three-unit" formula which Nehru said he "hated." [75] They believed that it would be more acceptable to the Maharashtrians, who were more threatening than the Gujaratis, and they believed that the leaders of the Gujarat PCC, who could be obdurate in intraparty negotiations, would have to yield to a parliamentary ground swell in favor of bilinguism, and might, in fact, welcome the opportunity to do so.

Congress contributed to the ground swell. Parliament's "big bilingual" plan was nothing more than the Maharashtra PCC's "big bilingual" plan with the five-year "option" to Gujarat left out. The "big bilingual" plan was supported by Congressmen in Parliament, most critically by leaders of the Bombay PCC, who were having second thoughts about life in a "third unit." It was also supported by C. D. Deshmukh, who had become a martyr to the Marhattas' cause. T. R. Deogirikar credits the Congress whip in the Lok Sabha, Satyanarayan Sinha, with being in the small multiparty group of parliamentary leaders who "conceived the idea" for circulating a petition among M.P.'s which called for the creation of a bilingual state. More than two hundred signed, and it was these signatures which

---

73. *Free Press Journal,* 5 October 1959.
74. For a sample of editorial comments see *Express,* 27 August, *Tribune,* 28 August, *Hindu,* 13 November 1959.
75. *Lok Sabha Debates,* vol. 10, part 2, 14 December 1955.

gave the government its opportunity to reintroduce the "big bilingual" formula as an alternative.[76]

In sum, a joint effort in which leaders of the non-Communist opposition played a leading role enabled the Congress-Government elite to make a decision that it probably wanted to make but could not make without help from outside. Although there were to be hard times ahead for Congress, "big bilingual" Bombay turned out to be by far the lesser of two evils. Had the "three-unit" scheme been adopted, trouble would have been avoided in Gujarat. But had elections and by-elections gone as they did in the Marathi-speaking areas of Bombay — and they might very well have gone worse, since Nehru's "three-unit" scheme was hated even more than the "big bilingual" formula — Congress's position in the Maharashtra "unit" would have been most precarious. Congress would have emerged from the general elections with a wafer-thin majority in the legislative assembly, 123 to 118, which it would have lost by 1960 through by-election defeats. There is no record of Nehru's expression of gratitude to the non-Communist opposition in Parliament for this service to Congress. But when the "big bilingual" formula's irremedial failure became apparent, Nehru and other Congress leaders attempted to facilitate their evasion of sole responsibility and blunt the Samyukta Maharashtra Samiti's attack by insisting that others share the blame for an idea that didn't work.[77]

The idea that did work, the bifurcation scheme of 1960, also came, in part, as a facilitative oppositional input. The input grew out of Pandit Pant's taunt to the opposition to come forward with a more acceptable solution than "big bilingual" Bombay, to do better than Congress (and Parliament) had done. The Samyukta Maharashtra Samiti and the Mahagujarat Janata Parishad took up the challenge and initiated in Poona in November 1957 a series of joint meetings to "negotiate" a scheme for the creation of Samyukta Maharashtra and Mahagujarat.

The first meeting was their most successful. The parishad renounced "in principle" Gujarat's objection to Bombay city's becoming the capital of Samyukta Maharashtra and secured from the samiti in return a promise of territorial and financial compensation for Mahagujarat. But at subsequent meetings they failed to work out

76. Deogirikar, *Twelve Years in Parliament*, p. 218.
77. See for example, Nehru's letter to Indulal Yajnik, in *Express*, 2 August 1957.

the details of this exchange. Their joint "ultimatum" to Congress in the form of a detailed bifurcation formula was not presented to the 1958 budget session of Parliament, as Indulal Yajnik had threatened, or to any subsequent session.[78]

It seems clear that these negotiations failed because, in effect, the Maharashtra PCC intervened, either tacitly or explicitly, to indicate to the samiti that bifurcation was inevitable and that it should make no unnecessary concessions to the Gujaratis. Particularly at issue was Dangs, a timber-rich, tribal area between Surat district of Gujarat and Nasik district of Maharashtra. In 1951, after two official surveys, Dangs was attached to Maharashtra, and thereby became Gujarat irredenta.

At Poona, the samiti agreed to "reopen" the question of Dangs.[79] "Reopen," in this context, could only mean a preliminary agreement to concede the area rather than a mere statement of willingness to discuss the matter. It was reasonable that part of Gujarat's compensation for renouncing its claim to first territorial prize, Bombay city, and thus making negotiations possible would be second territorial prize, Dangs. But, according to parishad negotiators, when they met with the samiti for the second time in Bombay city in January 1958, the samiti negotiators reneged on their agreement.[80]

Harihar Khambolja, one of the parishad negotiators, contended that between the Poona and Bombay sessions, the chief minister, Yashwantrao Chavan, let it be known through his "lobby" in the samiti, Datta Deshmukh of the Peasants and Workers party, that it would be unnecessary to concede Dangs to get Samyukta Maharashtra.[81] Whether or not Maharashtra PCC influence entered the negotiations through this route, it seems certain that it entered at about this time. S. M. Joshi reported that he began to see bifurcation as inevitable, and thought that concessions would be unnecessary to get it.[82] Samiti leaders belittle the importance of the issue of Dangs as a stumbling block to an agreement, and take the position that the negotiations were an end in themselves. But the public record suggests that at the time of the Poona meeting they no less than the leaders of the parishad anticipated presenting Congress

78. *Free Press Journal,* 8 and 18 November 1957, *Hindustan Standard,* 5 December 1957.
79. Joint statement, 5 November 1956.
80. Indulal Yajnik and Harihar Khambolja, interviews.
81. Interview.
82. Interview.

with an agreement, and that it was only after the Bombay meeting that Dangs became a public issue between the samiti and the parishad.[83] The samiti's representative in Parliament, Naushir Bharucha, had given notice of his intention to reopen the issue of Bombay reorganization, but was instructed, after the samiti-parishad meeting in Bombay, not to press the issue. According to a samiti spokesman, the time was not "opportune" and there was "now a greater realization even in the Congress ranks that the Bombay issue would have to be reopened." [84]

The "negotiations" between the samiti and the parishad were inherently difficult. Neither party had the capacity to effect any agreement. Both, their stock-in-trade uncompromising provincialism, were particularly sensitive to being charged with making unjustifiable concessions in order to reach an "opportunistic" agreement. Business support for the parishad virtually evaporated after it conceded Bombay city to the Marhattas, and the president of the Maharashtra PCC responded to the samiti-parishad joint statement on their Poona meeting by saying that "to Congressmen . . . the issue of Dangs is no more open to discussion." [85] The samiti and the parishad could only sow for the Congress to reap. The bifurcation settlement approved by the Congress Working Committee in 1960 was the settlement that the samiti and the parishad had failed to conclude in 1958: Bombay city to Maharashtra and financial and territorial compensation, *including Dangs*, to Gujarat.

The samiti and the parishad in 1957 picked up the negotiations which had been dropped by the Gujarat and Maharashtra PCCs when they were compelled to live together as good Congressmen in "big bilingual" Bombay. When, having failed, the PCCs began to negotiate a separation in 1959, they had the benefit of the political soundings taken by the samiti and the parishad and they applied to

83. It was Joshi who referred to the agreement as an "ultimatum." As early as September, before the Poona meeting, Dange warned that "very soon Congress and Parliament will be faced with an agreement"; *Hindustan Standard*, 24 September 1957.

84. *Free Press Journal*, 13 March 1958. It might be noted that Chavan, just two weeks earlier, had said in a public statement that Congress was "not thinking in terms" of reorganizing Bombay; *Bombay Chronicle*, 26 February 1958. But in retrospect, it seems clear that Nehru and Pant were beginning to drift in this direction at about this time, and that the leaders of the Gujarat PCC were making strenuous efforts to keep them on course; see statements of Morarji Desai, Khandubhai Desai, and Thakorbhai Desai in *Free Press Journal*, 26 April 1958.

85. *Hitavada*, 7 February, 1958.

their negotiations the framework that the samiti and the parishad had constructed for theirs. Pandit Pant, defending the financial compensation which Maharashtrian Congress negotiatiors had agreed to pay to the new Gujarat state, addressed himself to Samyukta Maharashtra Samiti critics with a characteristic acknowledgment of a facilitative oppositional input: "When they [the samiti and the parishad] did not settle the details, the burden fell on us of giving effect to the principles which had been accepted by them." [86]

Autonomous Associations and Political Parties

The Akhil Bharatiya Swarnakar Sangh or its state units might have thrown in their lots with one or more opposition parties. The Jana Sangh, for example, would have welcomed them with open arms. But the leaders of the Swarnakar Sangh were disinclined to accept such an arrangement. They had too little to bargain with: neither a regional base nor an extensive constituency. And such an arrangement could only have been an unequal one to the disadvantage of the smiths. In addition there was among the *swarnakars* a general distrust of politicians. There was also a realization that the sangh's internal cohesion and its capacity to deal with Congress would be adversely affected by too close a tie with any particular opposition party or with opposition parties in general.

Leaders of the Swarnakar Sangh were in part fearful that too close a tie with any political party would put them in jeopardy of having their organization "taken over" by politicians. The sangh was not unlike a trade union federation, although most of its members were self-employed artisans and it resisted their proletarianization. It was conceived by trade unionists, Jaswant Singh and the other leaders of the Delhi Goldsmith Workers Union, an INTUC affiliate. And its leaders thought of it as a protective association for "work-

86. *Lok Sabha Debates*, 2d series, vol. 41, 1 April 1960. One other attempt by the opposition to make a facilitative input should be mentioned in passing. This was the so-called Ashok-Harris plan. Named for its formulators, Ashok Mehta and Moinuddin Harris, it was a plan for local autonomy for Bombay city within unilingual Maharashtra. Like the "big bilingual" formula, it was an attempt by anti-Communist Praja Socialists to settle the Bombay question without a Communist alliance. The plan was much discussed, but was never accepted by either the Congress or the samiti.

ers" not only against government but against the "capitalist class" of "exploiters," the *sarafs* and jewelers. In India, the usual pattern is for trade unions to be "taken over," if not organized by politicians. The major trade union federations, and individual unions like the Girni Kamgar Union in Bombay, are affiliated with and dominated by particular political parties, which regularly use them for partisan political purposes. In resisting too intimate a tie with any particular party, the Swarnakar Sangh was resisting being so used.

In their initial encounters, smiths and politicians were in no small measure guided by stereotyped images of each other. As artisans, skilled craftsmen, creators of things, goldsmiths often manifest the same disdain for the politician's role as they do for the jeweler's — a disdain for the entrepreneur, the broker, the "uncreative" manipulator of things and people. Politicians of almost all parties, several of whom supported the smiths' fight against the rules, in return scorned the traditional "dishonest workman" or the contemporary smuggler. Jaswant Singh reported that in their early contacts with politicians, the smiths were not infrequently rebuffed, sometimes by those who later spoke in their support. These experiences reinforced their stereotype of politicians and convinced them of the wisdom of their initial decision to be politically independent. The perceived alternatives were using politicians or being used by them.

For the sangh, political independence was the sine qua non of internal cohesion. This was made apparent at its first meeting. The 150 goldsmiths who came to Delhi in February 1963 were members of most of the political parties in northern India. Had the sangh affiliated with any of them it would have risked sacrificing the support of goldsmiths who were adherents of the others and fragmenting the movement into a number of goldsmith groups attached to several parties. One of the first rules adopted by the sangh was a rule of official partisan neutrality. Thus, the sangh would not officially support Manilal's candidacy on the Jana Sangh ticket in 1967 for the legislative assembly seat from Tankura, a village close to Rajkot. Even in so small a place as Rajkot the goldsmiths were not a politically homogeneous group. Manilal's candidacy was supported only as a "courtesy" to a kinsman by the house of Khushaldas Dayalji, whose members are Congressmen and local Congress officials.

The sangh's decision to restrict its top leadership posts to members of goldsmith castes was, in part, a corollary to the decision to remain free of party connections. By establishing caste group membership as a criterion for leadership positions and forming a politically heterogeneous national leadership group, the sangh hoped to minimize the relevance of the partisan identities of its leaders and project the impression of nonpartisanship. It was important not only to *be* nonpartisan, but to appear to be nonpartisan. By and large the sangh was successful in this. Although its opponents, particularly among the *sarafs* and jewelers, complained that the sangh's Revolutionary Socialist general secretary, Anil Basu, was taking the organization in a "communistic" direction, they could not associate the sangh with any political party, and certainly not with the Revolutionary Socialist party, a group limited to West Bengal, or with the Communists, who were thought to have been originally in favor of the rules. Aside from providing the sangh with a structure which served to identify its leaders with it and to reduce the salience of their identification with political parties, caste also provided the sangh with resources of political skills, sophistication, and time which do not exist in great abundance among artisans who are bound to their tools. Caste also provided the sangh with leaders who had the appropriate status and English-language skills to plead its case in the national political arena.

Political independence not only enabled the Swarnakar Sangh to keep open its lines of communication to the various groups in the fragmented and mutually antagonistic opposition, it also facilitated its courtship of Congress sympathies. Affiliation with an opposition party or even with a coalition of opposition parties which could merely harass Congress would have been a liability. Congress leaders undoubtedly would have stigmatized the goldsmiths' organization as simply another vehicle to discredit Congress in the hands of "opportunistic" opposition parties. To stigmatize opposition in this way often seems to be a reflexive action of Congress leaders, even when, as in this case, it is clearly unwarranted. Thus, the finance minister, after three years of agitation against the rules by *goldsmiths*, observed that the rules had become a "political issue" and asked, rhetorically, who it was that was pressing for their annulment: "certainly not the disemployed goldsmiths who after three years of its [the rules] operation had found alternative means of employment." [87] Beyond being merely half-truths, statements such as these reflect not only a certain indifference to the interests of or-

87. *Hindustan Times,* 17 May 1966.

dinary people, but a contempt for their political capacities and an exaggerated view of the capacities of political elites to manipulate them. In both cases in this study these have been costly attitudes for the Congress-Government elite. If the smiths were scorned, the scorn was requited. Undoubtedly, antagonism for Congress grew apace among the goldsmiths between 1963 and 1966. It was on the lips of every one of the many goldsmiths who were interviewed for this study. But the leaders of the Swarnakar Sangh knew that they could not afford to alienate Congressmen; that the route to the Congress-Government elite who alone could change the rules would have to be through them.

The strategy of the sangh was to approach politicians without regard to their political affiliations. It sent delegation after delegation of smiths to call on M.P.s in New Delhi. To friendly M.P.s it supplied information to enable them to plead the goldsmiths' case in Parliament. This service is perhaps most graphically illustrated in the minute of dissent attached by a group of Congressmen to the report of the Joint Committee of Parliament on the Gold (Control) Bill of 1963. The minute is little more than a distillation of Anil Basu's pamphlet *Whither Gold Control?* It contains the same arguments, many of the same recommendations, and many of the same examples.[88] The sangh encouraged its state units to call on M.P.s in their constituencies, and to call on M.L.A.s and other prominent local and state politicians. All twenty or so M.P.s who were interviewed for this study reported that they had been called on by goldsmith delegations at least once, that many of their colleagues had also been called on, and that they were impressed with the goldsmiths' articulateness and organization.

The principal service that the Swarnakar Sangh asked of opposition politicians was to publicize the goldsmiths' cause and their distress, in Parliament and at public meetings called for those purposes. A heterogeneous group of politicians were almost always invited to the sangh's meetings, and not infrequently asked to address them. For example, at its meeting in August 1963 those invited included: Raj Narain, chairman of the All-India Socialist party; V. G. Deshpande, president of the All-India Hindu Mahasabha; P. Ramamurthi, a Communist M.P.; Balraj Madhok, president of the Delhi state Jana Sangh; and Abdul Ghani Dar and M. S. Aney, Independ-

88. Lok Sabha Secretariat, *The Gold (Control) Bill, 1963 (Report of the Joint Committee)* (September 1964).

ent M.P.s.[89] Agitation, however, was considered to be a job for
goldsmiths. Shankar Prasad Das, Jaswant Singh's successor as president of the Delhi Goldsmith Workers Union, reported that the
sangh had turned down an offer from Mani Ram Bagri, a socialist
M.P. whom the goldsmiths found helpful, to court imprisonment
during one of its "direct action" campaigns. There were thousands
of goldsmiths who were willing to go to jail, and the sangh was not
interested in being used as an agency to make martyrs of anyone
but smiths.[90]

Like the Swarnaker Sangh, the All-India Sarafa and Jewellers associations were organized independently of any political party or parties. But in their fight against the rules they had greater difficulty in
remaining free of political attachments. In large part this was because they could not elicit the same sympathy across party lines as
could the smiths. Many small *sarafs*, calling themselves "goldsmith-
dealers," as indeed they are, attempted to court general sympathy
as artisans and petty traders who had been displaced no less than
the "self-employed" smith, and had been discriminated against to
boot by the "fourteen-carat concession." But the leaders of the Sarafa Association, not to mention the Jewellers Association, were prosperous urban merchants, and their plight, such as it was, was hardly
apparent.[91] The Communists, of course, would have no part of
them and even among Jana Sanghis they were regarded as "big people" in contrast to the smiths, whom the Jana Sangh regarded as
part of its constituency.[92] Too, the jewellers' inclinations, bred not
only of necessity but of past experience, were to address their appeals not to a mass audience but to the "right people."

Leaders of the Swarnaker Sangh would never name a particular
party as being most helpful. In contrast, the secretaries of the Sarafa and Jewellers associations did not hesitate to so designate the

89. *Express*, 26 August 1963.
90. The sangh claimed that five thousand smiths had been arrested in its agitation campaign in New Delhi and other cities in August and September 1967.
In New Delhi alone one thousand were arrested, *Hindustan Times*, 27 August
1967.
91. In the winter of 1967 I attended the two-day celebration of the wedding
of one of Delhi's leading jewelers. In aesthetic terms, it compared favorably
with similar affairs conducted in the catering halls of Long Island and West-
chester County, but in terms of conspicuous consumption and conspicuous
waste it could hardly have been surpassed.
92. U. M. Trivedi, M.P., interview, New Delhi, 3 November 1966.

Swatantra party. The Sarafa Association enlisted the assistance of the Forum of Free Enterprise, a Bombay-based organization with close Swatantra connections devoted to propagandizing the virtues of private ownership.[93] The forum listed as one of its major activities in 1966 helping the Sarafa Association's "publicity and public relations campaign" against the rules.[94] Specifically, the forum helped the Sarafa general secretary, B. S. Mahajan, with his pamphleteering, and in December 1966 it held a public meeting in Bombay at which the featured speaker, S. G. Pethe, a leading jeweler of the city, roundly condemned what remained of the rules and denounced the government for promulgating them in the first place. M. R. Masani, the Swatantra general secretary, was an outspoken critic of the rules in Parliament and perhaps more than any other politician in 1963 made the rules an issue in his by-election campaign. The Swatantra M.P. Dahyabhai V. Patel provided his home in Delhi as a meeting place for *sarafs* and M.P.s and was active in Masani's campaign in Rajkot.

Like the smiths, however, and for the same reasons, the *sarafs* could not afford to alienate Congress. In addition, as businessmen, not infrequently dependent on the favors of politicians, they could ill afford to offend the leaders of the ruling party for reasons of their individual as well as collective welfare. In May 1966 the Sarafa Association scheduled a meeting in Bombay to coincide with the session of the AICC, and chose as its principal speaker Babubhai Chinai, a leading industrialist, an opponent of the rules, and a Congress member of the Rajya Sabha. When Congress president K. Kamaraj, at the Bombay session of the AICC, gave what was generally taken as his assurance that the rules would be scrapped, it was the president of the Sarafa Association who rushed to garland him and pronounced him to be the savior of "thousands of poor workers."[95] In private conversations *sarafs* were less likely to wreath the Congress president in marigolds, but there was no doubt about his position as one of the "right people."

An observation suggesting further research might be made here. M.P.s who were officially classed as "Independents," those who

93. M. R. Masani, who was to become a leader of the Swantantra party, was one of the forum's founders. The forum, in turn, was one of the organizations most responsible for sponsoring the Swatantra party in 1959; Erdman, *Swatantra Party*.

94. *Report for the Year Ended June 30, 1966*.

95. *Statesman*, 24 May 1966.

were actually or formally unaffiliated with any party and those who were not affiliated with one of the major "national parties," played a disproportionately active role in opposing the rules. Several of these Independents, many more than their number in Parliament would warrant, either performed single services for the *swarnakars* and *sarafs*, attended their meetings as distinguished guests, or were cited by them as being particularly helpful. They were a politically mixed group — for example, Prakash Vir Shastri, Abdul Ghani Dar, L. M. Singhvi, T. K. Chaudhuri, S. M. Banerjee. It might also be noted that the sangh's rule of partisan neutrality did not prohibit it from supporting its own candidates who would run as Independents. The importance of these observations should not be exaggerated. The Swarnakar Sangh did not seek out Independents because they were Independents, and its rule of partisan neutrality, as we shall see, did not prevent goldsmiths from supporting partisan opponents of the rules. Nevertheless, political independence seems congruent with the sort of oppositional process that is being described here. For groups like the Swarnakar Sangh, it seems to provide access to the political process without their being "taken over" by opposition parties, or endangering their cohesion by becoming embroiled in opposition politics, or alienating Congress.

Although the opposition parties were united against the Gold Control Rules, there was, ironically, widespread agreement among them in support of the state- and nation-building goals of gold control. Smuggling was universally regarded as an evil, and gold hoarding and "the lure of gold" as impediments to economic development. But agreement among opposition politicians was no less universal that the rules, as such, had failed to achieve any of their anticipated goals, that their achievements, on the contrary, had been counterproductive, and that in pursuing them the government had committed an exploitable blunder.

Sympathy for the goldsmiths' plight was the unifying referent for opposition to the rules. From this referent two general lines of attack were launched: the smiths were the victims of an undesirable assault by the government on "traditional" society, and the smiths were the victims of a misconceived policy of modernization. Although individual politicians sometimes specialized in one line of attack rather than the other,[96] except as a matter of emphasis nei-

96. Contrast for example, the argument of Prakash Vir Shastri, in *Lok Sabha*

ther line can be associated with any particular party, and each party's particular emphasis suggests a combination of ideological and constituency orientations.

Those who attacked the rules as an assault on "traditional" society, an attack not infrequently coupled with acknowledgments in private that the smiths were "dishonest workmen," tended to stress such objections as the rules' allegedly adverse effects on the rural credit system and on traditionally sanctioned savings,[97] on "birthright" and on Hindu religion, on art and on artisanship.

The Jana Sangh, more than any other opposition party, emphasized this line of attack. It might be noted that following its support for the movement against the rules, in 1967 the Jana Sangh was in the forefront of the agitation campaign in favor of central legislation barring the slaughter of cows. For the Jana Sangh, the smiths and the smaller "goldsmith-dealers" are, particularly, its potential constituency, part of the "floating lower middle class" on whose support the party depends – a class whom modernization threatens not only with economic loss, but with proletarianization through "copying of the West," division of labor, machine-made ornaments, factories, and "showrooms." Not only did the engineering industry fail to absorb a "substantial number of these nimble-fingered workmen," as a spokesman for the Gold Control Board had predicted it would, but the smiths showed little inclination to be absorbed into industry. Jana Sanghis, in particular, took up the goldsmiths' arguments as such; for example, that fourteen-carat gold was too hard for them to work with their ordinary tools and that they were not laborers who could be shifted from one job to the next.[98]

The Swatantra party was perhaps the first opposition group to speak out against the rules.[99] Yet of all the opposition parties, the

---

Debates, 3d series, vol. 14 (5 March 1963), with that of Dr. L. M. Singhvi, in India, Lok Sabha Secretariat, *The Gold (Control) Bill of 1963: Report of the Joint Committee* (September 1964).

97. It is suggestive of how widely these sympathies are held that G. B. Kotak, the first chairman of the Gold Control Board and, of course, an advocate of the rules, expressed a sympathetic understanding of gold hoarding. Referring to the *Arthashastra*, he distinguished between prohibition and the rules as, on the one hand, an injunction against a traditional vice and, on the other, an injunction against a traditional virtue; interview, Bombay, 19 February 1967.

98. U. M. Trivedi, M.P., interview, New Delhi, 3 November 1966, and *Lok Sabha Debates*, 3d series, vol. 12, 20 February 1963. Balraj Madhok, interview, New Delhi, 21 October 1966.

99. The parliamentary board of the party denounced the rules on 13 January 1963, four days after they were announced.

Swatantra party was probably held in least affection by the leaders
of the Swarnakar Sangh. For them it was the party of "big people"
in general and *sarafs* in particular. Even in Rajkot, the *swarnakars*
regarded Masani as a candidate of opportunity, and most of their
support for him in 1963 was channeled through the local Jana
Sangh, which, according to most accounts, was chiefly responsible
for his victory.[100]

Although the Swatantra party expressed sympathy for the goldsmiths and indignation at their treatment by the government, it was
the party of the factory and "showroom" owners, and it tended to
argue its case against the rules accordingly; that is, that they represented a misconceived policy of modernization — a policy that was
of a piece within the ruling party's "socialist" mismanagement of the
entire economy. Gold hoarding and smuggling were merely consequences of the government's inflationary policy of deficit spending.
The rules were addressed to a symptom rather than an illness and
symptomatic treatment which took the form of further bureaucratic
intervention in the economy could only make the patient worse.[101]

As might be expected, restrictions on gold consumption, at least
initially, attracted some support on the left as a modernization strategy. Indeed, Morarji Desai reported that his announcement of the
rules had been one of the few times when his work had received
praise from Communists and Socialists.[102] But the praise was
short-lived. From the rules' first hostile reception in Parliament a
month after they were promulgated, Communists denounced the
government for controlling gold consumption by punishing the poor
smith while it not only left the great ill-gotten hoards of the wealthy
intact but offered them gold bonds with handsome dividends.[103] A
Praja Socialist, who described the wearing of gold, particularly by
men, as "vulgar," attributed the distress and dislocation caused by
the rules to the government's failure to precede their promulgation
with the necessary and desirable "social devaluation" of gold.[104]

Procedural as well as substantive arguments against the rules
were raised. The government's failure to consult with the gold

100. *Statesman*, 24 May 1963, and *Hindustan Standard*, 3 June 1963.
101. M. R. Masani, Minute of Dissent, *The Gold (Control) Bill of 1963:
Report of the Joint Committee.*
102. Interview.
103. For example, A. K. Gopalan, in *Lok Sabha Debates*, vol. 14, 5 March
1963.
104. Interview, New Delhi, 9 November 1966.

trade, its reliance on civil servants for information, and its lack of data on which to base policy were frequently cited. For example, L. M. Singhvi, in his minute of dissent to the joint committee report on the Gold (Control) Bill, noted that he had asked S. S. Khera, the secretary of the cabinet secretariat, whether the informal committee of civil servants, "experts," which had advised the government on the bill and which Khera had headed, had made a detailed investigation of the resources that would be necessary to rehabilitate the unemployed smiths. Khera's response, shocking to Singhvi, was "No. We were working purely by rule of thumb. We were limited by the time at our disposal."

Khera also revealed to hostile questioners on the joint committee that his informal group had consulted with the chairman of the Gold Control Board before making its recommendations, but with no one in the gold trade.[105]

The rules were attacked as an unwarranted use by the government of emergency powers, emergency powers granted to meet an external danger but used for domestic purposes. When the government answered these criticisms by turning the rules into legislation, there was criticism of the additional powers of enforcement granted under the law.[106]

The arguments above, first raised by opposition parties, were echoed with increasing boldness by Congressmen. Two months after the rules had been promulgated the situation was accurately summed up by a Swatantra M.P. who observed that opposition to the rules was providing one of those "rare occasions when the various groups in the opposition and I believe many on the treasury benches also, despite their whip, would be unanimous in their finding regarding the futility of the Gold Control Rules . . . ."[107]

What contribution did the opposition parties make to the oppositional process? What role did their opposition play in compelling the Congress-Government elite to substantially alter the rules? Some opposition politicians who were goldsmiths, like Anil Basu and many others on the local level, provided the smiths with organizational skills and some opposition and, of course, Congress politi-

105. India, Lok Sabha Secretariat, *Joint Committee on the Gold (Control) Bill of 1963: Evidence* (September 1964).
106. *Hindu*, 28 June 1963, and *Hindustan Times*, 6 July 1963.
107. *Lok Sabha Debates*, 3d series, vol. 13, 5 March 1963.

cians pulled strings for their constituents in the gold trade, for example, by facilitating rehabilitation loans. But the principal contribution of opposition parties to the process of opposition was to provide spokesmen for the gold trade with access to political arenas in which to fight the rules — Parliament and electoral constituencies. In these arenas, Congressmen were explicitly or tacitly drawn into supportive relationships with oppostion politicians and members of the gold trade, and the support which smiths and *sarafs* gathered in these arenas encouraged them to persist in their opposition to the rules.

Parliament was the central arena. Over the years the government's gold control policy was debated several times and provoked numerous hostile questions and spirited exchanges. Many of these hostile questions came from Congressmen, and in several instances Congressmen joined opposition members in asking the same questions. The line of battle was not between the Congress and opposition benches, but between the Ministry of Finance and the House. At no time did any member of the government outside the Finance Ministry or any leading Congressman rise in Parliament to defend either the rules or the bill.[108] For sustained periods of time spokesmen for the Finance Ministry, with no apparent support or encouragement from their cabinet colleagues or their party, were obliged to rationalize and explain away the rules' failures.

Morarji Desai's downfall was in Parliament, and his removal from the Union Cabinet was, in part, attributed by his critics in the Lok Sabha to his gold control policy. U. M. Trivedi, the Jana Sangh leader in the Lok Sabha, told the House (and the press) that gold control had "cost Mr. Morarji Desai his career," [109] and no one rose to challenge him.

The only real attempt to draw the associations in the gold trade into the decision-making process was made in Parliament by the Joint Committee on the Gold (Control) Bill of 1963. If the associations were not listened to in the joint committee, they were at least heard. The evidence that the joint committee collected and publi-

108. Debates or extended exchanges between ministry spokesmen and M.P.s took place on 5–6 March and 21 September 1963, 4 June and 21–22, 24 December 1964, 23 August and 2–3 September 1966; *Lok Sabha Debates*. Questions are listed in the summary that follows the record of each day's business in the *Debates*. Questions on or relating to gold control were asked in almost every session of the Lok Sabha held between January 1963 and September 1966.

109. *Lok Sabha Debates*, 3rd Series, vol. 37, 22 December 1964.

cized was overwhelmingly in opposition to the bill. Almost every opposition member of the committee attached a minute of dissent to its report. So did nine Congressmen.[110]

Two things should be noted about the parliamentary arena. First, it had two sides rather than three or four. The opposition parties did not become so involved in the dispute between goldsmiths and *sarafs* that they split into two groups, one proposing an alternative to the rules favorable to the smiths versus another proposing an alternative favorable to the *sarafs*. The main thrust of the opposition's argument was opposition to the rules, as such, in favor of a return to the status quo ante; that is, no "quality control." If the "fourteen-carat concession" was aimed at splitting the opposition in Parliament as well as the opposition in the gold trade, it failed in both places. The goldsmiths were willing to postpone their demand for *swarna-silpa* in favor of having the rules annulled, but in Parliament even the demand had little resonance. For the Swatantra party, *swarna-silpa* involved the extension of state enterprise and a blow against its constituency's interests. The left was sympathetic with the smiths but concerned with the "social devaluation" of gold, a devaluation hardly likely to occur if *swarna-silpa* were to reduce the domestic price of gold. The Jana Sangh, it should be remembered, was the party not only of the goldsmith but also of the "goldsmith-dealer."

Second, we can only speculate on the opposition's responsibility for facilitating and encouraging opposition to the rules from the Congress benches. But the situation suggests a measure of responsibility. One experienced M.P. observed that the Congressmen who were most outspoken in their opposition to the rules, such as the nine who signed the minute of dissent to the joint committee's report, were "real backbenchers." Important Congressmen, he continued, opposed the rules but remained silent.[111] Government leaders outside the Finance Ministry who presumably supported the rules

110. Although W. H. Morris-Jones makes only passing reference to joint committees as such in his *Parliament in India* (London: Longmans, Green and Co., 1957), the Joint Committee on the Gold (Control) Bill, or at least certain members of it, manifested that quality which he found in Indian parliamentary committees in general: "self-consciousness as a legislature, distinctive from and even standing against the executive," p. 264. In general, only bills that are "highly controversial" or of "exceptional importance or unusual complexity" are referred to joint committees; ibid., p. 231. See also B. B. Jena, *Parliamentary Committees in India* (Calcutta: Scientific Book Agency, 1966).

111. Interview, October 1966.

were equally silent. According to press reports the cabinet was divided and the Congress president, who was also silent, opposed them. Insofar as there was *any* leadership on the issue for "real backbenchers" it came from the opposition. This is not to suggest that Congressmen were led to opposition by opposition politicians or that the failure of Congress leadership was any less responsible for facilitating opposition within the ruling party than the leadership of opposition politicians. But it seems unlikely that the attack on the rules, an attack in which Congressmen took part, could have been so sustained, pointed, and embarrassing to the government had it not been led by some of the opposition's, and Parliament's, most articulate spokesmen.

In April and May 1963, twenty-eight assembly and seven parliamentary by-elections were contested. Many of these contests had been postponed because of the war with China in 1962. Congress won the great majority of these, but the press and the Congress organization focused national attention on three "prestige" parliamentary by-elections that Congress lost. So concerned was Congress with these losses that it appointed a special By-elections Committee of party leaders to investigate them, and it commissioned academic studies of the party's organization in the three constituencies.[112]

These three were "prestige" contests because in them Congress candidates, one a minister in the Union Cabinet, faced opposition leaders who were nationally known as eloquent and vitriolic critics of Congress: at Farrukhabad in Uttar Pradesh, Rammanohar Lohia, the mercurial leader and founder of the Indian Socialist party; at Amroha in Uttar Pradesh, Acharya J. B. Kripalani, the *ancien terrible* of Indian socialism and V. K. Krishna Menon's self-appointed nemesis; and at Rajkot in Gujarat, M. R. Masani, the general secretary of the Swatantra party and one of the right's most eloquent spokesmen.

Unlike opposition to "big bilingual" Bombay, opposition to the rules was not so salient an issue to opposition parties that it overshadowed all other considerations. In the three "prestige" constituencies all opposition candidates were supported by ad hoc anti-Congress coalitions in which the Jana Sangh played a leading role.

112. These studies, made by staff members of the Centre for the Study of Developing Societies, New Delhi, appear in the *Economic Weekly*, 22, 29 May and 19 June 1965.

But the Communists supported neither Kripalani nor Masani, who are old enemies.

No doubt, many and diverse things determined the results of these by-elections: poor Congress organization and factionalism, Hindu-Muslim antagonism in Amroha and caste rivalries elsewhere, local issues and discontents — the price of kerosine and sugar, administrative arrogance, taxes, shortages, and so forth. The rules were raised as an issue in all three. Lohia, Kripalani, and Masani had the support of local smiths and *sarafs*, and in Rajkot they were convinced that Masani owed his victory to them. To what extent opposition to the rules played a part in these Congress defeats is unknown, however. But for our purposes that is immaterial. What is known and material is that official Congress inquiries were made into the by-election defeats, and the Union Cabinet, the working committee, and ordinary Congress politicians were told not merely by the press *but by their own people* that discontent with the rules had played a significant part in Congress's defeat in all three constituencies. Opposition to the rules drew Congressmen, not as dissidents but as "message authenticators," [113] into temporary and tacit supportive relationships with associations in the gold trade and with opposition parties.

In Farrukhabad one newspaper explained Lohia's victory by observing that "the *seths* [businessmen], *sarafs*, the shopkeepers, the merchants, and the . . . Jana Sangh gathered under the banner of Indian socialism." [114] Ram Asrey Rai, who was deputed by the AICC to investigate the election defeat, reported that "public dismay at the enforcement of the Gold Control Order [i.e. rules]" had contributed to the Congress defeat.[115] In its report on Farrukhabad, the special Congress By-elections Committee agreed that "feelings against such measures as Gold Control . . . gave rise to general dissatisfaction." [116]

Mahavir Tyagi, a veteran Congressman and a former member of the Union Cabinet, who managed the party's campaign in Amroha, reported that the rules were partially responsible for the Congress's defeat there.[117] The president of the Uttar Pradesh Congress Com-

---

113. See below, chapter 5.
114. *National Herald*, 5 May 1963.
115. *Hindustan Times*, 29 August 1963.
116. All-India Congress Committee, *Byelections Committee Report* (Jaipur, 23 October 1963).
117. *Times of India*, 1 June 1963.

mittee agreed,[118] and the By-elections Committee also cited the rules as a cause for "public dissatisfaction" in Amroha.

M. R. Masani attributed his victory in Rajkot, in part, to popular dissatisfaction with the rules and support from members of the gold trade.[119] The *Statesman* reported that the rules, "above all," were the issue in the Rajkot campaign and that Masani gave the Congress "sleepless nights" with his attacks on them.[120] Jethalal Joshi, the defeated Congress candidate, told the By-elections Committee that the rules had been among the "primary causes" for his defeat,[121] and the committee concluded that "Gold Control created dissatisfaction in a section of the society which actively worked for the Swatantra party." [122]

For the smiths and *sarafs* there was a significant feedback from the parliamentary and electoral constituency arenas. Knowing that their cause had attracted attention and support, reading about themselves in the newspaper, and winning concessions and victories were for the smiths messages of encouragement to persevere in their campaign against the rules inside and outside Parliament House. A goldsmith of Shahdara, a leader of the Delhi Goldsmith Workers Union, who was carried by the agitation against the rules from parochial respectability down Parliament Street and then to jail, shook his fist in the direction of the capital. "They tried to ruin us," he said, "but we organized and we would not stop fighting, and we finally beat them."

118. AICC, *Review of Byelection Results* (August 1963).
119. *Free Press Journal*, 6, 31 July 1963.
120. 24 May 1963.
121. *Hindustan Times*, 23 July 1963.
122. AICC, *Byelections Committee Report*.

5   CONGRESS

Congress both cues the process of opposition and plays parts in it. In both cases discussed here oppositional groups formed and supportive relationships were established among them in response to specific Congress-Government policies. Dissident and dissenting-but-disciplined Congressmen joined these groups and entered into these relationships, and when they withdrew from them groups and relationships all but disappeared.

Congressmen entered into supportive oppositional relationships with members of other parties and nonparty groups because they had the same or complementary interests in opposing Congress-Government policies. Congressmen who were Marathas and Marathas who were not Congressmen shared many of the same interests in the establishment of Samyukta Maharashtra. Congress businessmen of Ahmadabad and Gujarati Praja Socialists and Communists had complementary interests in Mahagujarat.

The process by which Congress-Government elites make policy contributes to, if it does not encourage, dissent and dissidence among Congressmen. The Congress Working Committee and the Union Cabinet formulated their states reorganization and gold control policies ostensibly and explicitly on the basis of state- and nation-building criteria, and on the assumption that others, particularly their "loyal Congress soldiers," would follow. They were not entirely correct in this assumption. In the case of Bombay's reorganization there were elaborate consultations between the Congress Government elite and provincial leaders before the States Reorganization Bill of 1956 was presented to Parliament, but these provincial leaders were without exception senior Congressmen. The authority which high Congress position supposedly bestowed on these provincial elders to negotiate as plenipotentiaries for their regions really enlarged and distorted their images like a circus mirror. Their capabilities to inspire or compel obedience to agreements that they reached among themselves were really quite limited even among Congressmen, much less among others. Before the announcement of the Gold Control Rules provincial Congress leaders were not consulted, although they were expected to support the policy. The government consulted no one but its "experts." In both cases it was only after the policies were announced that Congress-Government elites came to grips with the limitations of their organization and the capacities of others to oppose them. Decisions announced by them with finality and for urgent reasons of state were then reluctantly opened for renegotiation or reconsideration. But they were opened only to Congressmen. Renegotiation and reconsideration were means not only to affect a situation but to reestablish Congress's control over it.

Dissident and dissenting-but-disciplined Congressmen played a crucial role in the renegotiations which led to the bifurcation of bilingual Bombay. They formed the link between the Congress-Government elite in its role as aggregator of oppositional interests, on the one hand, and the oppositional groups which articulate and penultimately aggregate oppositional interests outside the Congress "system" on the other. In western India dissident Congressmen, particularly those allied with the Samyukta Maharashtra Samiti, held the key to the restoration and continuation of Congress dominance. Dissenting-but-disciplined Congressmen performed this linking function less dramatically, but not necessarily with less effect. While dissident Congressmen held out the promise of restoring Congress's position, dissenting-but-disciplined Congressmen held out the threat of further weakening it.

Dissenting-but-disciplined Congressmen also acted as authenticators of messages from outside the Congress "system." The importance of the authenticator's role for the oppositional process (and for Congress) is suggested by Morarji Desai's assessment of opposition parties:

> Unfortunately, in our country the opposition does not consist of strong parties, any of which can hope to oust the Congress from power and get a majority, so that it can run the Government according to its own programme. It therefore develops a weakness and frustration which result in an attitude of irresponsibility. . . . But [the opposition parties'] real weakness arises from their attempts to make unhealthy alliances among themselves and their concentration on an effort to make the Congress unpopular and weak.[1]

1. Morarji Desai, *In My View* (Bombay: Thacker and Co., 1966), pp. 95–96.

This evaluation was not baseless then and is not now. It is not difficult to understand how Desai and his colleagues in the Congress-Government elite could dismiss opposition from outside the ruling party as "irresponsible" and "opportunistic." But opposition from within the party cannot be dismissed so readily. If after three years of loyal and efficient service as chief minister of a bilingual Bombay whose creation he accepted as an act of discipline, albeit not without reward, Yashwantrao Chavan reported that it was a failure, who could question either his judgment or his sincerity? In the case of the Gold Control Rules, Congressmen acting as message authenticators for their party played perhaps an even greater role in the oppositional process than they had in Bombay. At no time or place did the controversy over gold control seriously threaten Congress dominance. What was at stake, the messages brought back from the front by "loyal Congress soldiers" suggested, was the party's morale and amour propre.

Dissent, Dissidence, and the Reestablishment of Dominance

Groups of dissident and dissenting-but-disciplined Congressmen developed supportive relationships with interest groups and opposition parties in western India. The largest and most strategically placed dissident group was the Samyukta Maharashtra Congress Jana Parishad. The Jana Parishad had been founded in 1954 by Marhatta Congressmen in the non-Marhatta dominated Bombay city Congress organization. The Jana Parishad's purpose was to present testimony before the States Reorganization Commission in favor of Samyukta Maharashtra and the establishment of its capital at Bombay city, positions that were diametrically opposed to those of its parent organization, the Bombay PCC.

S. K. Patil, the Bombay PCC chief, had been satisfied with the multilingual status quo. In 1955 he supported the States Reorganization Commission's "balanced bilingual" formula as a reasonable alternative. When this was rejected by the Maharashtra PCC he accepted the Congress Working Committee's "three-unit" solution, and in 1956 when the "big bilingual" scheme was resurrected in

Parliament he was one of its most ardent supporters. For S. K. Patil and the Bombay PCC any fate for their city was preferable to its becoming the capital of a Marathi state. For the Samyukta Maharashtra Congress Jana Parishad no other fate was acceptable.

The Jana Parishad would have accepted the Maharashtra PCC's "big bilingual" formula as an interim arrangement. The formula's "option" to Gujarat was virtual assurance that Bombay would become a Maharashtrian city after a delay of only five years. When the Gujarat PCC and then the Congress-Government elite rejected it, however, the Jana Parishad would hear no more of compromises and delays. It had most to gain or most to lose from any settlement. Its city was the center of the conflict and its people, the "clerks and coolies" of the city, had allegedly suffered most from the lack of Marhatta control over Marhatta affairs. At the same time, the city and its Marhatta population were most vulnerable to a compromise solution. A separate Bombay city, that is, a Bombay city controlled by Gujarati business interests, was the Gujarat PCC's asking price for Samyukta Maharashtra. When the Maharashtra PCC in 1956 accepted the "three-unit" formula it paid under protest, but it paid. The Jana Parishad would have to be the protector of its own interest. And in its own interest, it could be content with nothing less than a guarantee that Bombay city would become the capital of Samyukta Maharashtra. The Congress-Government elite would include no such guarantee in its "three-unit" formula.

In December 1955, the Jana Parishad defied S. K. Patil and voted for a Praja Socialist-sponsored resolution in the Bombay Municipal Corporation which called for the incorporation of Bombay city in Samyukta Maharashtra. Because of its votes, the resolution passed.[2] The Jana Parishad leader, T. R. Naravene, a physician in the city and a deputy minister in the state cabinet, was subsequently given the choice by the chief minister, Morarji Desai, of either dissociating from the Jana Parishad or resigning from the cabinet. He resigned from the cabinet, "coming out as a martyr."[3]

The working committee instructed the Jana Parishad to disband, but it refused. And after Nehru announced on January 16 that the city would be separated from Maharashtra, the Jana Parishad left

2. *Bombay Chronicle*, 14 and 23 December 1955.
3. T. R. Deogirikar, *Twelve Years in Parliament: Democracy in Action* (Poona: Chitrashala Prakashan, 1964), p. 205.

the Congress. Attempts by Shankarrao Deo and H. V. Pataskar, the Union minister for legal affairs, to bring it back were unavailing.[4] If by reversing his order of preferences and supporting "big bilingual" Bombay in Parliament rather than the "three-unit" plan S. K. Patil hoped to win back the Jana Parishad, that effort was also unavailing. There was no "option" to Gujarat in Parliament's "big bilingual" formula, and besides, the time for compromise had passed, at least temporarily. A spokesman for the Jana Parishad insisted that it had only been "temporarily driven . . . out" of Congress, and that its "ideological loyalty" to the ruling party was intact.[5]

Dr. Naravene described the Jana Parishad as a "parallel" organization to the Maharashtra PCC, in the same way that the Bombay Citizens' Committee paralleled the Bombay PCC. Leaders of the Jana Parishad continued to meet with leaders of the Maharashtra PCC for several months after the Jana Parishad had officially left the Congress, and it heeded a request from the Maharashtra PCC not to recruit dissident Congressmen outside the city.[6]

In July 1956 Naravene announced that the Jana Parishad would cooperate with the Samyukta Maharashtra Samiti's efforts to confront the Congress with straight-fights on the issue of Samyukta Maharashtra in the second general elections. By the time it withdrew from the samiti, three and a half years later, the Jana Parishad's delegation to the legislative assembly from Bombay city was second only to Congress's.[7]

Unlike the members of the Jana Parishad, who fit in well with the Samyukta Maharashtra Samiti's left front, the Congress defectors to the Mahagujarat Janata Parishad were, like the parishad itself, a mixed group. There were members of the Congress Forum of Socialist Action like Gangaram Rawal, conservative academicians like Himatlal Shukla, opponents of land reform like Purshottamdas Patel, and businessmen like Chinubhai Chimanlal Seth. Taken together, however, dissident Congressmen were the backbone of the Mahagujarat movement. As the Nagarik Paksh, they ran the municipal corporation at the movement's center, Ahmadabad, and of the thirty-two Janata Parishad candidates elected to the Bombay Legis-

---

4. *Hindustan Standard,* 11 April 1956, and *Free Press Journal,* 6 May 1956.
5. *Bombay Chronicle,* 27 February 1956.
6. T. R. Naravene, interview, Bombay, 22 April 1967.
7. Five to eleven; *Times of India,* 22 December 1959.

lative Assembly in 1957, nineteen were dissident Congressmen. Of the five Janata Parishad candidates elected to the Lok Sabha in 1957, three were dissident Congressmen.[8]

Like the Congress dissidents of Bombay city, the Congress defectors in Gujarat made it known that they expected their estrangement to be only temporary. The Congress-Government elite's decision to bifurcate was barely a week old when in August 1959 Gangaram Rawal, speaking for the Gujarati dissidents, declared, "Our quarrel with Congress was only about the bilingual state. Now that the issue is being settled we shall go back."[9]

The Nag-Vidarbha Andolan Samiti attracted some prominent Congress defectors, notably M. S. Aney and Brijlal Biyani. But by and large it was less significant as an oppositional force than were the leaders of the Nagpur PCC, who were dissenting-but-disciplined.

While Congress dissidents chipped away at Congress's dominant position in western India, dissenting-but-disciplined Congressmen threatened to wear it away. Every crisis brought a new wave of disaffection which fell with greater impact than the one before it.

In November 1955, after the Congress Working Committee initially agreed to a "three-unit" formula (Bombay city to become a city-state) and violence and police firing followed, Congress M.L.A.s from Maharashtra met, and a majority of them threatened to resign rather than support the formula in the Bombay Legislative Assembly. Only by postponing the discussion was a crisis averted.[10]

Nehru's announcement on 16 January 1956 of the federally administered Bombay city variation of the "three-unit" formula, also followed by violence and police firing, provoked the resignation of C. D. Deshmukh and a call for resignations in protest from the executive committee of the Maharashtra PCC to all its M.P.s and M.L.A.s. This time the interventions of Nehru, who convinced Deshmukh not to press his resignation, and of the Congress Working Committee, which refused to accept the resignations of the M.P.s and M.L.A.s, were necessary to avert a crisis.

In April there was a minor crisis. Before the States Reorganization Bill was presented to the legislative assemblies for their opin-

8. Gangaram Rawal, interview, Ahmadabad, 22 April 1967.
9. *Free Press Journal*, 27 August 1959.
10. Deogirikar, *Twelve Years in Parliament*, p. 203.

ions and suggestions,[11] PCC presidents were instructed by the Congress general secretary that no member of Congress was to vote against the bill, or table or support any amendments to it, or abstain from voting without the permission of state leaders.[12] But when it appeared before the Bombay Legislative Assembly, Morarji Desai complained, twenty-three Congressmen voted against it and twenty-four moved amendments which they later voted for.[13] Most of these Congressmen were from Bombay city's neighboring coastal districts of Kolaba and Ratnagiri.[14]

Nehru's announcement in June that Bombay city's fate would be finally decided by a plebiscite *in the city alone* after a five-year period of central administration was followed by rioting and by new threats of mass resignations from the Maharashtra PCC. These were once again turned back. But C. D. Deshmukh did resign and T. R. Deogirikar, then president of the Maharashtra PCC and a member of the Congress Working Committee, attached his name to a minute of dissent from the recommendation in favor of the "three-unit" formula passed by the Joint Committee of Parliament on the States Reorganization Bill.

The eleventh-hour substitution in Parliament of "big bilingual" Bombay for the "three-unit" scheme was too little and too late to appease Maharashtrian Congressmen. The Maharashtra PCC had become factionalized over the reorganization issue; there was disagreement over what would be the best compromise solution, and even whether any compromise solution should be accepted.[15] The "big bilingual" scheme was finally accepted, but without enthusiasm and by a divided Maharashtra PCC. Any hope that it might eventually rally around the scheme, or at least live with it, was shattered by the results of the 1957 elections. One of the elections' messages was that loyalty to Congress in Maharashtra was not, under the prevailing circumstances, a key to political success. How much longer would the Congress-Government elite be able to contain dissatisfaction within party discipline when the discipline provided neither a refuge nor a reward and a functioning and successful alternative political organization, the Samyukta Maharashtra Samiti, was available?

11. Their approval is constitutionally unnecessary.
12. *Congress Bulletin*, circular no. 4 (March 1956).
13. Ibid., (April 1956).
14. *Hindu*, 7 August 1956.
15. Deogirikar, *Twelve Years in Parliament*, pp. 218–20.

In Nag-Vidarbha and Gujarat dissenting-but-loyal Congressmen were less menacing than they were in Maharashtra. But they nonetheless represented threats to Congress hegemony in western India. Nag-Vidarbha might have determined whether or not Congress would go into the new state of Maharashtra with a majority in its legislative assembly. In Gujarat after 1959, there was a question of how long the stern discipline of Morarji Desai and the tact and skill of Thakorbhai Desai could hold the dissenting businessmen and landholding peasants from the burgeoning Swatantra party, particularly if it were to do well in the 1962 general elections.

After the States Reorganization Commission submitted its recommendations for the reorganization of Bombay, the matter was formally renegotiated twice. The first renegotiation series began in October 1955 when the Congress Working Committee decided not to accept the States Reorganization Commission's recommendations for Bombay reorganization, and it culminated in the passage of the States Reorganization Act in August 1956. The second renegotiation series began in August 1959 and ended with the passage of the Bombay Reorganization Act in April 1960.

Congress's approach to renegotiations suggests its adherence to something approaching the following decision-making guidelines.

1. Decision making should remain a monopoly of disciplined Congressmen.

2. Since intraparty dissent is unavoidable in a democratic system, compromise is necessary in order to maintain this monopoly.

3. Although intraparty dissent is unavoidable, what should be avoided is the establishment of such supportive relationships between Congressmen and non-Congress oppositional groups which threaten Congress's decision-making monopoly.

4. When it becomes impossible to avoid this threat, then it is time to renegotiate.

5. Authoritative renegotiations, like the making of other political decisions, should be a monopoly of disciplined Congressmen and should have as a major objective the renovation or restoration of that monopoly.

It should be recalled that from the first appearance of linguistic-provincialism as a political issue for independent India, the Congress-Government elite has hedged. It took its stand, in principle, on "the unity of India" and it stressed the possible threat to unity of "provincialism." But when the demand for linguistic-provincial reorganization threatened Congress's dominant position, as it did initially in Andhra, then the Congress-Government elite negotiated. This was the pattern it followed in the controversy over the issue of Bombay reorganization.

Fully aware of the issue's potential for disruption, the working committee in April 1954 laid down ground rules for intraparty dissent. Because they illustrate so well our third guideline, they should be quoted in some detail:

> In the opinion of the [Working] Committee, all Congress Committees and Congressmen should have full freedom to represent their points of view. . . . In case of any differences of opinion, the minority in any Congress Committee should be free to represent its views.

> *But*

> It is expected that Congress Committees and Congressmen will not participate [in] or carry on agitation on this matter, nor will they associate with other parties in making joint representation to the [States Reorganization] Commission. Congressmen should not join in a common platform with other political parties in the expression of the views of Congressmen on this question. Congressmen cannot, in the very nature of things, carry on public agitations against each other on this subject.[16]

One month after these rules were announced, the Congress Working Committee was compelled by intraparty dissent to compromise on them. It gave B. S. Hiray, the leading Maharashtrian Congressman and the working president of the Samyukta Maharashtra Parishad, and S. Nijalingappa, the leading Congressman from Mysore and a member of the working committee, permission to do exactly what it had just forbidden, "to associate [their PCCs] with other parties in making joint representation to the [States Reorganization] Commission," and to "join in a common platform with other political parties in the expression of the views of Congressmen." [17]

In 1954 and 1955, the Congress president (Nehru), general secretary, and working committee felt it necessary to direct a number of pleas and warnings to Congressmen to avoid an "agitational approach" to the problem.[18] But the agitation continued. Marhatta

---

16. Indian National Congress, *Resolutions on States Reorganization, 1920–1956*, p. 7.

17. Ibid., p. 9.

18. *Congress Bulletin*, no. 2 (February–March 1954), Balvantray Mehta's circular no. 3, and PG–2/8/1920. Ibid. no. 4 (May 1954) and no. 5 (June–July

Congressmen had no reason to anticipate any pleasant surprises from the "experts" on the States Reorganization Commission. Its members "[already knew] the minds of the leaders at the top," Deogirikar observed, "how could they, even if they willed, paddle the ship against the current." [19] The commission's recommendations were greeted in Bombay with denunciations from Congressmen sharing a "common platform" with Communists and Praja Socialists, and they touched off violence. At its first meeting, on 13 October, two weeks after the States Reorganization Commission had submitted its report, the Congress Working Committee scrapped the commission's recommendation for a "balanced bilingual" Bombay.[20] It then opened the first series of renegotiations which were directed toward arriving at some generally acceptable variation of the "three-unit" formula. The "three-unit" formula became the basis for renegotiation when the Gujarat PCC rejected the Maharashtra PCC's "big bilingual" scheme and on the suggestion of Maulana Azad, Congress stalwart, peacemaker, and Union minister of education from 1947.

Several things should be noted about this first series of renegotiations. First, it was entirely an affair of Congress hierarchs. Second, these hierarchs could produce an agreement among themselves, but they could not translate this agreement into a settlement of the issue. Third, the Indian constitutional system felt the effects of the Congress-Government elite's penchant for limiting authoritative renegotiations to Congress hierarchs and for using renegotiations as a means of renovating Congress's dominant position. Finally, the renegotiations brought Yashwantrao Chavan, as a dissenting-but-disciplined Congressman, to political prominence.

The Language Subcommittee of the Congress Working Committee, officially appointed in November 1955 and composed of Nehru, U. N. Dhebar, Maulana Azad, and Pandit Pant, was *the* authoritative mediating, arbitrating, and policy-making body on states reorganization for Congress *and* the Government of India. It based its decisions on long and complicated consultations with "representatives of all the States concerned." [21] All these representatives, how-

1954), letters from Nehru. Indian National Congress, *Resolutions on States Reorganization, 1920–1956.*

19. Deogirikar, *Twelve Years in Parliament*, p. 188.

20. Ibid., p. 198.

21. Working committee resolution of January 1956, Indian National Congress, *Resolutions on States Reorganization, 1920-1956.*

ever, were provincial Congress hierarchs. Morarji Desai was the chief negotiator for Gujarat, S. K. Patil for Bombay city, and B. S. Hiray and Shankarrao Deo for Maharashtra.[22] Other Congressmen were invited to participate in these renegotiations. But non-Congressmen were not, and in January 1956 the Maharashtra PCC withdrew from the parishad entirely. The "big bilingual" plan which was eventually incorporated in the States Reorganization Act of 1956 was devised and supported by a multiparty group of M.P.s. But the decision to accept it was made in the Congress Working Committee after consultation with Congressmen.[23]

That the renegotiations could produce an agreement among Congress hierarchs but not a settlement of the issue suggests the limited control which these hierarchs have over their environments, even their Congress environments. Morarji Desai, who was generally regarded as the towering figure in the Gujarat Congress, gave his assent to Parliament's "big bilingual" plan in spite of clear warnings that the plan would not be acceptable to many Gujarati Congressmen who wanted a state of their own. The decision was not referred to the Gujarat PCC for its approval.[24] Presumably, Desai's assent was considered to be sufficient. After he had given it, he "declared that the decision was in the interest of all, it was irrevocable, and those who misbehaved would be severely dealt with." [25] But it didn't work. The formation of the Mahagujarat Janata Parishad with dissident Congressmen as its backbone and the threat of a right-wing renascence in Gujarat were part of the response.

A great deal of effort and energy went into negotiating a compromise agreement among the powers in the Maharashtra Congress — Hiray, Chavan, Deogirikar, Shankarrao Deo — but it was no more, but rather less, productive of a settlement than Desai's more preemptory approach. Congress's desire to retain its decision-mak-

22. Shankarrao Deo, to be precise, was not a dues-paying Congressman at the time. But this is not very meaningful precision. In the line of Gandhi and J. P. Narayan, to mention two more prominent recent examples, Shankarrao Deo was a highly respected, elderly politician formally outside his party but actually one of its leaders. He had been a member of the Maharashtra PCC for twenty-five years, its president, and general secretary of the national Congress. He was the originator of the Maharashtra PCC's "big bilingual" plan with its five-year "option" to Gujarat.

23. Deogirikar, Twelve Years in Parliament, p. 219.

24. Government of Bombay, Report of the Commission of Inquiry.

25. D. N. Pathak et al., Three General Elections in Gujarat (Ahmadabad: Gujarat University, 1966), p. 56.

ing monopoly put representational and leadership burdens upon it which it could not carry.

Congress guarded its decision-making prerogatives against incursions not only from other parties and nonparty groups but from parliamentary structures as well. C. D. Deshmukh cited as one of the two principal reasons for his resignation from the Union Cabinet the usurpation of its decision-making powers by the Congress Working Committee's Language Subcommittee. The "two crucial decisions" on the future of Bombay which were announced by Nehru in January and June 1956, Deshmukh maintained, were the Subcommittee's and not the cabinet's. With regard to the latter decision Deshmukh said,

> There was no consideration of the proposal in the Cabinet or even by circulation. There was no individual consultation with members of the Cabinet known to be specially interested, as for instance myself. There is no record even of a meeting of the Committee of the Cabinet and to this day no authoritative text of the so-called decision is available to members of the Cabinet.[26]

Nehru attempted to draw some of the sting from Deshmukh's accusation, in part by suggesting that Deshmukh had played a significant role in the renegotiations and that the cabinet had been consulted.[27] But U. N. Dhebar termed Deshmukh's description of the Language Subcommittee's role "correct." [28] Pant acknowledged in the Lok Sabha that the "three-unit" formula which provided the basic framework for renegotiations was a Working Committee product, and that Nehru made his statement in June after having consulted with "some friends." [29]

The Congress-Government elite attempted to control the votes of Congressmen on the Joint Committee of Parliament on the States Reorganization Act of 1956. Conventionally there is no party whip in such committees. Nehru's statement of 3 June, which had prompted Deshmukh to press his resignation, was made while the joint committee was sitting, and was widely interpreted and criticized as an instruction to its Congress members.[30] In the report of

26. *Lok Sabha Debates*, vol. 3, part 2, 25 July 1956.
27. Ibid., 30 July 1956.
28. Interview.
29. *Lok Sabha Debates*, vol. 7, part 2, 31 July 1956.
30. See, for example, the statements of C. D. Deshmukh in Ibid., 25 July 1956, and Lanka Sundaram, U. R. Bogawat, and S. S. More in Ibid., 26 July 1956.

the joint committee's proceedings specific reference is made to Nehru's statement.

According to Lanka Sundaram, who served on the joint committee, the government did not permit "free voting" among Congressmen on the joint committee, instructed them that they could not agree to anything that had not been approved by state and national Congress leaders, and thwarted the inclusion in the bill of a statutory boundary commission, although a majority of the joint committee's members wanted such an inclusion.[31] Acharya Kripalani said, "Activity from the whip of the Congress was going on all the time." [32] T. R. Deogirikar described the reaction of Pandit Pant to the minute of dissent which he and G. S. Altekar attached to the joint committee's report:

> Shri Pataskar [Union minister for legal affairs] came immediately to me and told me that Pant wanted to see me. . . . Shri Pant wanted me to withdraw the note of dissent. . . . I replied that I could not be true to Maharashtra and accept the Government proposal. . . . After our first day's talks, I was reminded that I was a member of the Working Committee and that any such statement would be detrimental to the cause of the Congress. . . . I was really sorry to displeasure Shri Pant after his great persuasion, but my duty ordained me [to act] otherwise. From that day onwards I ceased to get his compliments for piloting [Maharashtra] P. C. C. during hard times and for keeping it alive. We agreed to differ and I brought down on myself all the fury and wrath of the leaders at the top.[33]

According to Deogirikar he offered to resign from the working committee at this time, but his resignation was not accepted. 1958, however, was his last year as president of the PCC and member of the working committee. Dissent must be more than merely an embarrassment supported by words if it is to extort rewards rather than draw punishments. If Deogirikar's rash act suggests the limits of dissent, the performance of Yashwantrao Chavan during the first renegotiation series indicates the rewards of loyalty. It was during these months that Chavan rose to first place in Maharashtrian politics.

Chavan's rise is an event significant in itself. He is one of India's most capable politicians. And if any one man can lay claim to being the founder of Samyukta Maharashtra it is Chavan, "the new Shi-

31. Ibid., 26 July 1956.
32. Ibid., 30 July 1956.
33. Deogirikar, *Twelve Years in Parliament*, pp. 217–18.

vaji." What is of greatest interest here, and of greatest credit to his skill as a politician, is that he did this as a dissenting-but-loyal Congressman.

In December 1955, Chavan, then Bombay minister for local self-government, supported by two other Bombay ministers, declared that the time for an all-party approach to the problem of Bombay's reorganization was over. They would take their direction from the Congress Working Committee, then debating "three-unit" formulas, rather than from the upcompromising Samyukta Maharashtra Parishad.[34] Thus, very early in the first renegotiation series Chavan established himself as a moderate alternative to the militant B. S. Hiray, who was then the chief minister-presumptive of Samyukta Maharashtra. Chavan matched Hiray proffered resignation for proffered resignation, and his loyalty to the ultimate goal of Samyukta Maharashtra was never seriously questioned. But neither was his dedication to a Congress solution to the problem. The turning point in his and Hiray's careers came after Nehru's declaration of 3 June 1956 that Bombay city would be centrally administered for five years. Hiray led the rebellion by supporting the resolution in the Maharashtra PCC which gave "any responsible Congressman" permission to "relinquish, if necessary his official position in the Government" in order to openly support Samyukta Maharshtra.[35] Chavan led the loyalists. Hiray won the battle by a vote of sixty-six to fifty-six in the PCC. But Chavan won the war. "Chavan's stars came into the ascendent from that day, and . . . Hiray began to lose ground." [36] He lost it all shortly after the decision to create "big bilingual" Bombay was made and Morarji Desai asked to be selected by his Congress colleagues, unanimously or with near unanimity, as its first chief minister. Hiray insisted on a contest. Desai withdrew and gave his support to Chavan. "Shri Chavan got a majority of votes and Shri Hiray was defeated," writes Deogirikar. "Hiray's adherents, one by one, were won over to Chavan's side, and Hiray and his group became poor souls." [37]

As the chief minister of "big bilingual" Bombay, Chavan dutifully pronounced it to be the "final solution" [38] to the reorganization

34. *Free Press Journal*, 3 December 1955.
35. *Express*, 6 June 1956.
36. Deogirikar, *Twelve Years in Parliament*, p. 217.
37. Ibid., p. 227.
38. *Hitavada*, 15 December 1956.

question. But during the second renegotiation series, Chavan played a major role in dismantling it and establishing a Maharashtra state. He was first chief minister of that too, and apparently had little difficulty in asserting that he had been in favor of Samyukta Maharashtra all along.[39]

During the months which followed the creation of "big bilingual" Bombay, the Congress drifted inevitably toward a second renegotiation series. It was being seriously threatened from the outside with violence and electoral defeats. Inside, the dissenting-but-disciplined were becoming more outspoken in their demands for the dissolution of the bilingual state.

The new leaders of the Maharashtra PCC were under increasing pressure from below, where the 1957 elections had left political careers in shambles, to press for bifurcation. Hiray, supported by the president of the Nasik District Congress Committee, G. H. Deshpande, an election victim, was apparently attempting to ride the waves of Congress dissatisfaction back to power.[40] At the Nagpur meeting of the AICC, Nehru was petitioned to bifurate by a group of Maharashtrian Congressmen.[41]

To the east, pressure of a different sort was mounting. Dissenting-but-loyal Congress leaders of Nag-Vidarbha, dissatisfied with their lots in bilingual Bombay, were reviving the demand for Mahavidarbha. In 1959 almost every Congress group in Nagpur resolved itself in favor of a separate Nag-Vidarbha. The Nag-Vidarbha Andolan Samiti and M. S. Aney were more active than ever. M. D. Tumpalliwar, an important "erstwhile Vidarbhite" in the Nagpur PCC, began to backslide toward Mahavidarbha.[42] In March 1959 Brijlal Biyani began such a vigorous and outspoken campaign in favor of Mahavidarbha that he was expelled from the Congress Legislative party after forty years of service as a party and government leader in central India.[43]

S. K. Patil "had ceased to be a hurdle in the way" of the dissolution of Bombay.[44] Only his former allies in the Gujarat PCC clung to

39. Bombay, *Legislative Assembly Debates*, vol. 10, part 2, 14 March 1960.
40. *Free Press Journal*, 15 September 1958. U. N. Dhebar, among others, was critical of Chavan for not taking Hiray into his cabinet.
41. Ibid., 1 January 1959.
42. *Hitavada*, 16 February 1959.
43. Ibid., 29 March 1959.
44. Deogirikar, *Twelve Years in Parliament*, p. 297.

the bilingual state. Only if they stayed in Bombay could the Gujaratis keep their milch cow, and, perhaps, only if they stayed in Bombay could Gujarati politicians aspire to positions of power and influence in the national Congress organization. In an "interview" quoted by a Gujarati Praja Socialist, Morarji Desai was alleged to have said that "all the Congress leaders came from big provinces," and he therefore "wanted the province [Bombay] to remain big so that its leaders may wield power." [45] Gujarati Congressmen, no less than Praja Socialists, partially attribute their PCC's fondness for bilinguism to Morarji Desai's ambitions.[46] To be sure, neither Desai nor the Gujarat PCC was alone in favoring a big province for its political potential. The leaders of the Bombay PCC were reluctant to be confined to their island stronghold. K. K. Shah, the president of the Bombay PCC, was quoted in 1958 as favoring bilingual Bombay as a "balancing force" and a "cover to small states" against the potential for national dominance of Uttar Pradesh, India's most populous state.[47] In 1956, S. K. Patil had joined with Morarji Desai in supporting the merger of Rajasthan, Maharashtra, and Gujarat in a *Paschim Pradesh* (western province) — a very big province.[48] By 1959, however, the Bombay PCC had paid a heavy price for not yielding to the demand for Samyukta Maharashtra, but in Gujarat the Janata Parishad was fading and the Swatantra party was merely a cloud on the horizon.

It was the Gujaratis who were the staunchest advocates of consolidating the six PCCs in Bombay state into one, in the hope of giving the bilingual arrangement some permanent foundation.[49] This was accomplished superficially by reducing the PCCs to Regional Congress Committees under one statewide Bombay PCC. But there was opposition, particularly in Maharashtra and Bombay city, to any organizational change other than in name. Thakorbhai Desai, a leading figure in the Gujarat Congress, was the first and last president of the statewide Bombay PCC. It was, he said, "never a reality." [50]

Nehru vacillated. In a letter to Indulal Yajnik and in a speech

45. Sanat Mehta in Praja Socialist Party, *Report of the Fourth National Conference* (Poona, 25–28 May 1958).
46. Interviews, Ahmadabad.
47. *Statesman*, 27 September 1958.
48. *Times of India*, 24 January 1956.
49. Bombay, Maharashtra, Gujarat, Marathwada, Nagpur, and Vidarbha.
50. Interview, Ahmadabad, 28 April 1967.

at Aurangabad in Maharashtra in August 1958, Nehru suggested that the bilingual arrangement was mutable. "It is open to Parliament to revise any decision." [51] On the basis of this and similar oracular statements, a member of the Bombay Legislative Assembly withdrew his bifurcation resolution and declared that he was "satisfied." [52] He was no doubt puzzled by the report in September that the working committee had decided "finally" *not* to reopen the issue and instead to create a single PCC in Bombay state to "set at rest all rumors regarding a move to split up the bilingual set-up." [53]

Supporters of the bilingual arrangement reported that they expected to meet with Nehru before the Hyderabad meeting of the AICC in October "to impress on him the need to give a firm verdict" in favor of its perpetuation.[54] Apparently he was not impressed. The creation of the bilingual state was a "correct decision," he said at Hyderabad, but there was no point in his saying that "nothing in the world can change that decision." [55]

The drift continued for the next few months, but its direction became more and more discernable. In November Nehru told a press conference that a change could not be "ruled out absolutely." [56] In December he told an audience in Ahmadabad that although he personally did not like "unilingual provinces," there was no question of "high principle" involved.[57] In a letter to Nag-Vidarbha Congressmen, made public in July 1959, he said quite firmly that he opposed the establishment of Mahavidarbha.[58] In August, the second renegotiation series opened.

Although it is not completely clear at whose initiative the reorganization question was reopened in 1959, there is no doubt that the second renegotiation series, like the first, was a Congress affair. Indira Gandhi, then Congress president, was credited in some reports for taking the initiative.[59] According to U. N. Dhebar, Ra-

51. *Hindu*, 31 July 1958, and *Bombay Chronicle*, 20 August 1958.
52. *Free Press Journal*, 17 September 1958.
53. Ibid.
54. *Hindustan Standard*, 17 October 1958.
55. *Congress Bulletin*, nos. 10 and 11, (October–November 1958).
56. *Free Press Journal*, 8 November 1958.
57. *Express*, 19 December 1958.
58. *Hitavada*, 20 July 1959.
59. Deogirikar, *Twelve Years in Parliament*, p. 297, and *Free Press Journal*, 28 August 1959.

jendra Prasad, the president of India, on the basis of his observations in Maharashtra and his conversations with political leaders there, suggested to Nehru that reorganization be seriously considered.[60] Pandit Pant told the Lok Sabha that the principal reason for reopening the issue was Chavan's report that "the greater unity which was to be forged through reorganization had not been achieved." [61]

The first more-or-less formal session of the second renegotiation series took place in Delhi in August.[62] The participants, according to Nehru's report, were the members of the Congress Working Committee's Language Subcommittee, minus Azad, who was dead, and Morarji Desai and Yashwantrao Chavan, the concerned provincial Congress hierarchs.[63] The basic decision to bifurcate was probably made at this first meeting. At the Chandigarh meeting of the AICC in September, Mrs. Gandhi appointed a committee of nine senior Congressmen to renegotiate a reorganization settlement. Pant, who as home minister had guided the working committee's reorganization decisions through Parliment, was chairman. The other members were interested Congress leaders. They included the regional "big three": Chavan and Jivraj Mehta, the chief ministers-designate of Maharashtra and Gujarat, and S. K. Patil; Thakorbhai Desai, the president of the stillborn statewide Bombay PCC; K. K. Shah, the president of the Bombay (city) RCC and lately a more outspoken opponent of bifurcation than S. K. Patil; G. R. Khedkar, a former president of the Vidarbha PCC and a consistent supporter of Samyukta Maharashtra, M. S. Kannamwar, former president of the Nagpur PCC and an on-and-off supporter of Mahavidarbha; and Savanakar, the president of the Marathwada RCC.

The committee of nine appointed a subcommittee of two, Chavan and Jivraj Mehta, to work out the division of disputed territory and financial assets between Maharashtra and Gujarat. In December the Working Committee gave its approval to the settlement that they had reached. Then, according to Pant, "This matter was taken up by Government and the Government have proceeded on

60. Interview.
61. *Lok Sabha Debates*, 2d series, vol. 41, 31 March 1960.
62. According to one report it was "common knowledge" that it took place at Pant's residence on 22 August; *Free Press Journal*, 31 August 1959.
63. *Free Press Journal*, 5 October 1960.

the basis of the agreement reached between the [Congress] leaders of the two States." [64] With the possible exception of the meeting between Nehru and S. M. Joshi in November 1959, the opposition parties played no formal part in the second renegotiation series. In December 1959, Nehru dismissed S. M. Joshi's suggestion for a multiparty meeting to demarcate the borders between Maharashtra and her neighbors as "not feasible." [65]

The bifurcation of Bombay was treated by Congress, to quote Jivraj Mehta, as a "family partition." [66] The negotiators were family elders. Although each was interested in maximizing his own share of the family fortune, they all shared a common interest in recouping it and in assuring that its future disposition would remain in their hands. Maharashtra was to be the principal legatee of bifurcation, and to Chavan fell the task of incorporating that legacy into a settlement that would excite neither jealousy nor dissatisfaction within the family. The second renegotiation series was permeated with that familial spirit which Chavan described as "give and take." [67]

The Bombay (city) RCC described itself as "unhappy" over the decision to bifurcate, but promised, as a group of "loyal" Congressmen, to accept it.[68] It had little to lose. Ironically, events over the preceding eighteen months had strongly suggested that it was only in Samyukta Maharashtra that the Gujarati-dominated Bombay Congress was likely to regain control of the city. And this was what it bargained for in the second renegotiation series. It wanted to be restored to the rank of PCC. And it was, the only "enclave" PCC in Congress. The Nagpur, Vidarbha, and Marathwada RCCs were absorbed into the Maharashtra PCC. It wanted its dissidents back under its wing and the Jana Parishad was told by Chavan that there would be no Samyukta Maharashtra unless it returned.[69] It wanted the "cosmopolitan character" of the city preserved, special attention paid to its developmental needs, and English to remain the medium of instruction at Bombay University, to be replaced, if at all, by Hindi rather than Marathi. Chavan gave his public assurances

64. *Lok Sabha Debates*, 2d series, vol. 41, 31 March 1960.
65. *Amrita Bazar Patrika*, 4 December 1959.
66. Deogirikar, *Twelve Years in Parliament*, p. 297.
67. *Free Press Journal*, 13 December 1959.
68. *Hindu*, 15 September 1959.
69. Interview, T. R. Naravene.

that these demands would be met.[70] Implicit in Chavan's assent to these last, apparently innocuous demands was the assurance that the economic and political status quo in the city would not be disturbed. The anticapitalist rhetoric of the Samyukta Maharashtra movement was to have no programmatic consequences. No fewer than three members of the Bombay Citizens' Committee accepted positions in Chavan's first cabinets. And to complete the task of reconciliation in the city, so did the Congress Jana Parishad leader, T. R. Naravene, who left the Bombay cabinet as a deputy minister and returned to the Maharashtra cabinet as a minister (of prohibition). P. K. Sawant, who led the rebellion of Congressmen from the coastal districts bordering the city against the "three-unit" formula and who was the party whip in the Bombay assembly in April 1956, came into the cabinet as minister of agriculture.

The Nagpur RCC was in an anomalous bargaining position. Its preference for a separate Mahavidarbha had, if anything, grown as a result of its experiences in bilingual Bombay. And it may be remembered that the Mahavidarbhites in 1956 preferred a composite state to Samyukta Maharashtra. In October 1960, Mrs. Gandhi was confronted with the threatened resignation of most of the Congress M.L.A.s from Nagpur, and the possibility that M. S. Kannamwar would quit Congress's nine-member committee [71] unless the demand for Mahavidarbha were met. Yet it could not be met. But because it could not be met, and for the same reasons, particular attention had to be paid to reconciling the Mahavidarbhites to Samyukta Maharashtra.

Mahavidarbha could not be created. First, because the leaders of the Vidarbha Congress wanted to come into Samyukta Maharashtra, and the four districts of Nagpur could not stand alone as a separate state. Second, even if it had been possible to convince the Vidarbha leaders to go into Mahavidarbha, the Congress-Government elite would not have created it. Congress's majority from the Marathi-speaking areas in the Bombay Legislative Assembly came from Nag-Vidarbha and Marathwada. To separate Mahavidarbha would have been to establish Maharashtra with a non-Congress majority in its first legislative assembly and, more than likely, to perpetuate that majority by creating an irredenta in Nag-Vidarbha.

70. Bombay, *Legislative Assembly Debates*, vol. 10, part 2, 14 May 1960.
71. *Deccan Herald*, 30 October 1959.

Congress, to paraphrase an old antagonist, does not operate as a political party in order to preside over its own dissolution.

On the other hand, because it provided Congress with its majority, and majorities may be lost, Nag-Vidarbha had to be reconciled to Samyukta Maharashtra rather than forced into it. There was some bitterness in Nag-Vidarbha because, as Nehru acknowledged, it "had to be persuaded" to join "big bilingual" Bombay,[72] and without support from Nag-Vidarbha, Congress's future in Samyukta Maharashtra was at best uncertain. Could Congress recapture Maharashtra? The signs were not all reassuring. For example, it lost the district board elections in Ratnagiri *after* the decision to bifurcate had been made and was known.[73] Although it was widely alleged that in their November 1959 meeting Nehru and S. M. Joshi had discussed the possibility of Congress-Praja Socialist cooperation as an alternative to a Congress-majority government in a Maharashtra without Nag-Vidarbha, this was certainly not a preferred alternative for Congress, and, in any event, no such agreement seems to have been reached. Joshi postponed his "irrevocable decision" to resign from the Samyukta Maharashtra Samiti *after* his talks with Nehru.

Chavan's efforts at reconciliation in Nag-Vidarbha were prodigious. That he is a Maratha-Kunbi and that Maratha-Kunbis account for about 20 percent of the population in Nag-Vidarbha no doubt helped. To Nag-Vidarbha, in general, he publicly pledged to implement the Nagpur Pact, including the provision for an annual meeting of the legislative assembly in Nagpur city, and to supplement it. To the large neo-Buddhist community, which had thrown in its lot with the Andolan Samiti, went his assurance that the benefits of official discrimination in their favor which they had enjoyed before their conversion from Hindu scheduled castes would be returned to them. To the Koshti weavers went his promise of help in establishing a cooperative spinning mill to give them some control over the price of yarn and some protection from Bombay city. To the peasant proprietors went time to adjust their holdings to meet the provisions of the Bombay Tenancy Act.[74] To make assurances doubly sure for the Brahman lawyers of Nagpur, the government

72. *Bombay Chronicle*, 30 August 1958.
73. *Times of India*, 24 December 1959.
74. Bombay, Ministry of Law, *The Bombay Tenancy and Agricultural Land (Vidarbha Region and Kutch Area) (Amendment) Act of 1962.*

agreed to incorporate into the Bombay Reorganization Act the Nagpur Pact provision for the establishment of a high court seat at Nagpur city. Finally to the Congress politicians of Nag-Vidarbha went positions of power and prestige. Chavan was more sensitive to the problem of unemployment among politicians than Morarji Desai would be to the problem of unemployment among goldsmiths. Of the fourteen ministerial positions in Chavan's first administration, five were held by politicians from Nagpur and Vidarbha. M. S. Kannamwar was given second place in the cabinet and succeeded Chavan as chief minister in 1962. He was succeeded at his death in 1963 by V. P. Naik from Vidarbha, who was also brought into the cabinet by Chavan. G. B. Khedkar from Vidarbha was elected president of the Maharashtra PCC in 1960 and was given third place in the state government in 1962. So successful was Chavan in rallying dissenting-but-loyal Congressmen in Nag-Vidarbha to Samyukta Maharashtra and in weakening the Nag-Vidarbha Andolan Samiti that he could safely ignore dissidents like Aney and Biyani.

The heart of the settlement was, of course, the division of Bombay's financial assets and disputed territories between its two successor states, Maharashtra and Gujarat. In making these divisions Chavan and Jivraj Mehta followed the guidelines that were set out by the Samyukta Maharashtra Samiti and Mahagujarat Janata Parishad in their negotiations: Bombay city to Maharashtra and compensation to Gujarat.

The question of how much Maharashtra should pay Gujarat to compensate it for the loss of revenue from Bombay city's surplus required some "expert" consultation and advice. But the final decision, in effect to "split the difference" between the Bhattacharya Committee's "expert" estimates of Gujarat's normal budgetary deficit and its "irreducible" deficit, was made by Jivraj Mehta and Chavan with Pant's assistance.[75] The territorial settlement was made without "experts," in the best spirit of a "family agreement," and on the "principle of proceeding with the greatest goodwill." [76] The elaborate, documented, and published territorial claims which had been made before the States Reorganization Commission and its predecessors by the Maharashtra PCC, through the Samyukta

75. *Free Press Journal,* 17, 23, 25 February 1960.
76. B. N. Datar, minister of state in the Ministry of Home Affairs, in *Lok Sabha Debates,* 2d series, vol. 43, 19 April 1960.

Maharashtra Parishad, and the Gujarat PCC and its allied organizations, were simply set aside.[77] Basically, the bifurcation line adopted was the line already known and accepted by the "family" elders, the jurisdictional line dividing the Maharashtra and Gujarat PCCs. Compensatory adjustments in favor of Gujarat were made from this line.

Gujarat's major compensation was the teak forests of Dangs. Nothing so well illustrates Congress's use of negotiations as a means of reestablishing its dominance through compromise among its factions than the disposition of Dangs. In 1949 the two leading politicians in multilingual Bombay, B. G. Kher, the chief minister negotiating for the Marhattas, and Morarji Desai, the home minister negotiating for the Gujaratis, agreed that Dangs had greater linguistic affinity with Maharashtra than with Gujarat. In 1951 the "expert" committee headed by Dr. Bakshi Teckchand concurred. The Election Commission then dutifully detached Dangs from Surat district in Gujarat and attached it to Nasik district in Maharashtra. The Census Commission "experts" gave the arrangement their blessings by finding in their 1951 enumeration that 95 percent of the Danghis spoke Marathi, whereas in previous censuses they had been able to find no more than 10 percent of the Danghis who spoke Marathi.[78]

In spite of this "settlement," Dangs became part of Gujarat irredenta. In its Memorandum to the States Reorganization Commission the Gujarat PCC dismissed the "Kher-Morarji award" as a "summary inquiry" and in spite of Morarji Desai's preeminence, disowned it.

In the Congress Working Committee's aborted "three-unit" for-

77. The parishad claimed taluks in Belgaum and Karwar districts of Mysore, in Surat district of Gujarat, in districts of Hyderabad outside Marathwada, and in districts of Madhya Pradesh outside Nag-Vidarbha; *Reorganization of States in India*. None of these claims were included in the bifurcation agreement. Aside from Dangs, the Gujarat PCC claimed six taluks in West Khandesh district and the Umbargaon taluk of Thana district in Maharashtra, and a small area in Rajasthan; *Memorandum*.

78. The Census Commission had come to its 1951 figure by listing as Marathi-speakers those whom previous censuses had listed as speakers of Bhili, a tribal language. Compare for example, the language tables in *Census of India, 1951*, Paper no. 1, Languages–1951 Census, Dangs District, and *Census of India, 1921*, vol. 7, part 2, Bombay Presidency. In its memorandum to the States Reorganization Commission, the Gujarat PCC strenuously objected to the 1951 figure. But, in 1961, with Dangs safely back in Gujarat, the Census Commission reduced its Marathi-speakers to the usual 10 percent; *Census of India, 1961*, District Census Handbook 17, Dangs District.

mula of 1956, Maharashtra "lost" Bombay city and was compensated with Dangs. In 1960, it was Gujarat's turn to be compensated. It "lost" Bombay city and in the Jivraj-Chavan award it got Dangs. Chavan justified this "arbitrary gift" for whose giving the Congress had earlier criticized the Samyukta Maharashtra Samiti by treating the victory of a Gujarati Congress faction in Dangs district board elections in 1959 as a virtual plebiscite. The samiti did not regard the elections as a plebiscite and Chavan need not have either except for the principle of "give and take." It should be noted that the other territories which had been in dispute between Maharashtra and Gujarat and were slated to be part of Maharashtra's compensation in 1956 — parts of West Khandesh district and villages in Umbargaon taluk of Thana district in Maharashtra — went to compensate Gujarat in 1960.

Maharashtra's border controversy with Mysore was simply left unsettled, and here, as in the case of the Maharashtra-Gujarat border controversy, the Congress-Government elite refused to apply any standard criteria of border demarcation, such as the so-called Pataskar formula, where the village is taken as the demarcation unit, or to agree to the appointment of a statutory boundary commission. In the Lok Sabha debate on the Bombay Reorganization Act a Communist M.P. referred scornfully to the "principle" on which the boundary line between Maharashtra and Gujarat had been drawn: "That principle is the agreement between Shri Chavan . . . and Shri Mehta . . . , [a] principle of bargaining." Pant, summing up the case for his government, did not disagree:

> My own feeling throughout has been, and still continues to be, that a settlement between the [Congress] leaders is the best method of solution of these border problems or other problems.[79]

Congress, Democracy, and Gold

Unlike the issue of linguistic-provincialism in western India, the issue of gold control created no Congress dissidents and no immediate, and probably no long-range, threat to Congress's dominant position anywhere. Congress critics of the rules were, of course, an embarrassment and an annoyance, but all remained within the let-

79. *Lok Sabha Debates*, 2d series, vol. 43, 19 April 1960.

ter if not the spirit of party discipline. They joined opposition politicians in Parliament and on public platforms to criticize the rules, they attached their signatures along with members of other parties to hostile questions directed at the finance minister, and nine Congressmen joined the unanimous nonconcurrence of opposition members with the Joint Committee of Parliament's report on the Gold (Control) Bill of 1963 by attaching to it a separate minute of dissent.[80] The government had no reason to fear, however, that disciplined Congressman would threaten its decision-making monopoly by establishing supportive relationships with opposition politicians. In the Congress whip's one test on gold control, the vote on the Gold (Control) Bill in December 1964, not a single Congressman crossed the floor. Although in debate the measure was almost universally opposed by those Congressmen who spoke, at the division they either voted "aye," as did two of the signatories of the Congressmen's minute of dissent to the joint committee's report, or they didn't vote.[81]

In by-election compaigns, Congressmen did not defend the rules. The Congress's special By-elections Committee reported that opposition "propaganda against [the rules] was built up far out of proportion to the facts." But that "Congressmen . . . did not do much to counteract this . . . probably out of lack of conviction on their own part." But neither did Congressmen defect on the issue to join opposition coalitions. Congress was not threatened at the polls. During April and May 1963, when Congress lost its three "prestige" by-elections, it won twenty-four parliamentary and legislative assembly contests of the thirty-five held. In those that Congress lost, although the By-elections Committee cited the rules as a contributing factor — and of all central legislation *only* the rules and the compulsory deposit scheme [82] — it concluded that factionalism and poor organization in the local Congress units were the principal causes for defeat. The Congress-Government elite's annulment of the "fourteen-carat rule" on the eve of the fourth general elections, a leisurely process which began in May 1966 and was terminated in

80. There were ten such minutes signed by a total of twenty members of the joint committee.

81. The vote was 209 to 62; *Lok Sabha Debates*, 3d series, vol. 37, 24 December 1964.

82. A scheme for forced savings adopted during the Sino-Indian crisis of 1962.

November, is best understood as part of a general fence mending in anticipation of a hard campaign rather than as a response to a particularly threatening situation.

But although Congress leaders had little reason to feel threatened by the rules, they had no reason to feel pleased. Outside the Finance Ministry and its "expert" advisors, support for the rules among Congressmen at all levels was minimal and constantly decreasing, until by 1966 it had evaporated. According to G. B. Kotak, with the exception of "half a dozen" people in the government "no one took [the rules] seriously." [83] In August 1966 a Congress M.P., on the floor of the Lok Sabha, said that Congress opinion in favor of "scrapping" the rules was "unanimous," and no one rose to challenge him. [84]

What was the contribution of dissenting-but-disciplined Congressmen to the process of opposition against the government's gold control policy and to the formation of supportive oppositional relationships with opposition parties and interest associations in the gold trade?

It was suggested earlier that the Congress-Government elite made what must be considered a major contribution to the development of supportive relationships among the rules' opponents. They abdicated from leadership. The rules announced by Morarji Desai on 9 January 1963 had been discussed and approved by the prime minister and his colleagues in the Union Cabinet. According to Desai, although the rules were his "brain wave" he had been asked to prepare such a policy by Nehru, and when the policy was discussed in the cabinet some colleagues expressed opinions in favor of even more stringent restrictions on gold consumption than those in the original rules. [85] Yet neither Nehru nor his successors, nor any member of their governments outside the Finance Ministry ever rose publicly to defend the government's gold control policy. Nehru's one public intervention into the controversy over the rules was to speak to a large gathering of goldsmiths who were demonstrating against them in front of his New Delhi residence in May 1963 and to leave them with the impression that he had "personally and pub-

83. Interview.
84. Kamalnayan Bajaj in *Lok Sabha Debates*, 23 August 1966, mimeographed.
85. Interview.

licly assumed responsibility for rehabilitating us." [86] When this impression was "supplemented, endorsed, and ratified" by two letters from his private secretary, the Akhil Bharatiya Swarnakar Sangh lifted its eleven-day-old *dharna* and expressed its "deepest sense of gratitude to the Prime Minister." [87] It is unlikely that the finance minister, who was arguing that reports of mass unemployment among the smiths were "very much exaggerated" [88] and that agitation would "merely confuse the issue," [89] felt equally grateful. The failure of Nehru and the cabinet to come to his and the rules' assistance, a failure which he attributes to "political dishonesty," is a source of bitterness for Morarji Desai.[90] Mrs. Tarkeshwari Sinha, who was Desai's deputy minister, put the blame for the failure of the government's gold control policy squarely on the shoulders of the government and Congress leaders who refused to support it.[91]

Throughout the controversy, the national Congress-Government elite was divided over the rules. So divided that it delayed a year between introducing the Gold (Control) Bill in Parliament and bringing it to a vote; and even after it had been passed into law, the government did not publish it in the *Gazette of India* — an extraordinary omission.[92] Only in 1968 was gold control as an act of Parliament so published and thus brought into force, without the "four-

86. Akhil Bharatiya Swarnakar Sangh, *Whither Gold Control?* (Calcutta, n.d.).
87. Ibid.
88. *Lok Sabha Debates*, 3d series, vol. 12, 20 February 1963.
89. *Hindu*, 11 July 1963.
90. Interview.
91. Interview.
92. This was the best and most generally accepted reason for the government's failure to notify the act. Another suggested reason was the government's fear that the bill's constitutionality could be successfully challenged in court. The procedure for constitutional amendment in India, however, was such that a united, determined government commanding a 75 percent majority in Parliament could have beaten back such a challenge, as it had done in the past. See M. V. Pylee, *Constitutional Government in India* (Bombay: Asia Publishing House, 1960). In 1967, however, in the case of *Golaknath* v. *State of Punjab*, the Supreme Court, in a landmark and highly controversial decision, declared that the "fundamental rights" guaranteed by the Indian constitution cannot be abridged even by constitutional amendment; V. N. Shukla, *The Constitution of India*, 5th ed. (Lucknow: Eastern Book Co., 1969). In April 1969 the Supreme Court upheld the constitutionality of the Gold Control Act, but declared that the power of regulation conferred on the administrator under the act was excessive and that some of his regulatory powers were in violation of the "fundamental right" under the constitution to carry on a trade. On 30 August, the Government of India promulgated an ordinance "virtually restoring" the act; *Conparlist* 1 (May 1969): 9, and 1 (June–July 1969): 17.

teen-carat rule." Throughout the period of this study the policy was enforced under the rules, although the bill was explicitly introduced in 1963 as a means of establishing the government's commitment to gold control and the bill passed into law in 1964.

The secretary of the Sarafa Association reported that his organization received an assurance from the home minister, Gulzari Lal Nanda, that when Lal Bahadur Shastri, Nehru's successor, returned from his talks with the Pakistanis and Russians in Tashkent the issue of gold control would be "reopened." [93] Shastri, of course, never returned. Mrs. Gandhi's government was divided on the question of what to do about the rules. Her finance minister, Sachindra Chaudhuri, like his predecessors, favored their retention. But by August 1966, opinion within the national Congress-Government elite had turned overwhelmingly in favor of the rules' annulment or substantial modification, and when the cabinet failed to agree on the necessary revisions an emergency meeting of the Congress Working Committee was called at which it was recommended that the "fourteen-carat rule" be annulled.[94] As early as February 1966, it was reported by a leading Congress M.P. and printed in an official Congress publication, the working committee had resolved that the rules had "outlived its purpose and utility." [95]

Some leading members of the party's inner circle – the "syndicate" – barely concealed their disapprobation of the rules. S. K. Patil, the leader of the Bombay PCC, did not conceal his at all. Two months after he, along with Morarji Desai, among others, was forced from the Union Cabinet under the so-called Kamaraj Plan, Patil dubbed the rules a failure.[96] Atulya Ghosh, the chief of the West Bengal PCC, could bring himself to say nothing kinder about the rules than that they were "necessary when [they] were promulgated." [97] When Morarji Desai threatened to close the mines at Kolar Gold Fields in Mysore as part of the attack on gold, S. Nijalingappa, then chief minister, warned against creating even more unemployment.[98] Congress President Kamaraj said nothing publicly but was widely regarded as no supporter of the rules, and,

93. Interview.
94. *Statesman*, 26 August 1966, and interviews.
95. Babubhai Chinai in *Congress Bulletin*, April–June 1966.
96. *Deccan Herald*, 17 November 1963.
97. *Hindustan Standard*, 13 July 1963.
98. *Hindu*, 12 June 1966.

to quote a fairly typical observation, he "made no secret of his distress at the extreme hardship caused to the goldsmiths." [99]

It was on Kamaraj's implied assurance that the rules would be modified that a resolution asking the government to annul them was withdrawn from the Bombay meeting of the AICC in May 1966. A man of few words, Kamaraj was quoted as having said no more than "it [the rules] is under consideration of the Government." [100] That was enough. In August, a Congress M.P., chiding the government for still retaining the rules, said, "It was very much debated in the All-India Congress Committee session [at Bombay] and we were given an understanding [from Kamaraj] that a decision will be taken soon in favor of scrapping the Gold Control Order." [101] No doubt it was Kamaraj's intervention that spared the government the embarrassment of having its gold control policy repudiated by the AICC. One observer noted that "AICC resolutions should influence Government policy; but they do not. Both State and Central Governments regard the sessions . . . as entertaining jamborees and occasions to watch the strengthening or decline of State and national factions." [102] Nevertheless, had the rules been repudiated by the AICC, it seems likely that the government's burden would have been increased substantially.

The rules were involved in Congress's "palace politics." But the effect of this involvement on their disposition, although not insubstantial, should not be exaggerated. That Morarji Desai was one of the central figures in the case lends itself to this sort of exaggeration. He is no doubt the most persistently controversial figure in the top echelon of Congress leaders, and not for his policies alone but for his personality as well.[103] Perhaps this has contributed to his perception of politics in general and the politics of gold control in particular as a play of characters rather than a play of issues. Those who opposed his gold control policy, according to Desai, either suffered from some personal failing or were motivated by antagonism for him. His best explanation for the "fourteen-carat concession" of Sep-

99. *Tribune,* 3 September 1963.
100. *Free Press Journal,* 23 May 1966.
101. *Lok Sabha Debates,* 23 August 1966, mimeographed.
102. *Patriot,* 17 May 1966. Stanley A. Kochanek assigns a more significant role to the AICC meetings, *The Congress Party of India* (Princeton, N.J.: Princeton University Press, 1968).
103. For a good recent biographical sketch, see Joseph Lelyveld, "The Karma of Morarji Desai," *New York Times Magazine,* 24 September 1967.

tember 1963 was that it was an attempt by Krishnamachari to dis-
tinguish himself from Desai. Why else should Krishnamachari become conciliatory toward the goldsmiths as finance minister when
as minister for economic and defense coordination in 1962 he had
been a supporter of even tighter restrictions on gold consumption
than those incorporated in the original rules? [104] Then, would it be
any less valid or productive to ask: Why other than out of pique at
being "Kamarajed," or to discredit his successor, did Desai as former finance minister announce that the "fourteen-carat concession"
had so weakened the rules that "there was no point in discussing
them" and that he favored their abolition? [105]

The point is not that personal antagonisms among Congress hierarchs have no explanatory value — of course they do — but that they
should not be permitted to obscure the realities of the issues for the
analyst even if they do obscure them for the principals. Desai's han-
dling of the issue, his unwillingness to compromise, his insensitivity
to the interests of the gold trade, his lack of foresight, were, by any
standards, unfortunate. It was to these real problems that Krishnamachari, whatever his motivations, addressed his concesssion to the
smiths. In terms of the gold control "scenario" the "fourteen-carat
concession" was ill-advised and destructive, and Desai's criticism of
it, whatever his motivation, was well taken. But Krishnamachari, no
less than Desai, was and remained a staunch advocate of gold control. The Gold (Control) Bill which he presented to Parliament and
kept alive in the joint committee provided both for putting the rules
on a permanent foundation and for stiffening the restrictions on the
gold trade and on gold consumption. One observer of the bill accused Krishnamachari of "out-Desaing Mr. Desai." [106] Sachindra
Chaudhuri, Krishnamachari's successor, defended the rules to the
bitter end.[107] The thankless job of defending the rules became in-
stitutionalized in the Finance Ministry. None of the finance ministers enjoyed the public support of his cabinet colleagues on the unpopular measure, and with one exception the alignment of Congress
opinion against the rules was apparently unaffected by the personality or tactics of any particular finance minister.

104. Interview.
105. *Free Press Journal*, 24 May 1964, and *Hindu*, 29 April 1966.
106. *Pioneer*, 29 November 1963.
107. According to one newspaper account, it was because of Chaudhuri's
defense of the rules in the Cabinet that the emergency meeting of the Working
Committee, referred to above, was called; *Statesman*, 26 August 1966.

The one exception, as was suggested above, was Krishnamachari's "fourteen-carat concession." What the concession did was to ally Congressmen who initially opposed the rules and those, like Morarji Desai, who supported the rules initially but opposed the concession. The chief spokesman for the nonofficial resolution introduced at the Bombay AICC session calling upon the government to abandon the rules was Mrs. Tarkeshwari Sinha — the same Mrs. Sinha who as deputy minister of finance under Morarji Desai had shared with him the onerous job of defending the rules in Parliament. Her attack on the rules at Bombay, accompanied by cheers and general approval, was an amalgam of sympathy for the "thousands of honest, poor goldsmiths" whom the rules had deprived of "their sole means of livelihood" and annoyance at the government for having "watered . . . down" the rules with the "fourteen-carat concession." [108]

Although, at least initially, the states were expected to bear the burden of providing "rehabilitation" funds and services for the smiths who became unemployed as a result of the rules, state Congress leaders were not, in general, consulted beforehand, and they resented the imposition of an unwanted and unpopular burden. G. B. Kotak, in discussing the attitude of provincial Congress leaders toward the rules, quoted one chief minister as having said that the rules were "Morarji's baby, not mine." Explicit or implied criticism of the rules came from party leaders in Kerala,[109] Madras,[110] Bombay,[111] and Assam.[112] P. G. Kher, president of the Bombay PCC and chairman of the reception committee for the May 1966 meeting of the AICC, took the extraordinary step of including in his welcoming address a call for the repeal of the rules "as early as possible." [113]

Among ordinary Congress politicians there is no doubt that the rules were widely opposed and resented. From his interviews with 108 Congress M.P.s, Henry Hart reports that they probably received a larger quantity of constituent reactions to the Gold Control Rules than they did to any other government policy during

108. *Free Press Journal*, 24 May 1966, and *Congress Bulletin*, April–May 1966, pp. 213–17.
109. *Free Press Journal*, 5 September 1963.
110. *Hindu*, 29 April 1966.
111. *Free Press Journal*, 31 January 1963.
112. Ibid., 4 June 1963.
113. *Hindustan Standard*, 22 May 1966.

1963–64.[114] As was the case in Maharashtra, what was a matter of
"prestige" at the top, an unwillingness to bow to a combination of
pressure and reason, was a matter of careers in politics at the bottom. Two contributions of Congress opponents of the rules to the
formation of supportive relations with other oppositional groups
might be noted here. First, Congress opponents of the rules contributed to the united front against them. In general, Congressmen, like
their counterparts across the Lok Sabha's aisles, did not divide
publicly on possible alternatives to the government's policy. They
simply opposed "quality control." Although the minute submitted
by the nine Congress dissenters from the report of the Joint Committee on the Gold (Control) Bill repeated the Akhil Bharatiya
Swarnakar Sangh's demand for *swarna-silpa* as an alternative to the
status quo ante, this alternative was never pressed by any of them.
Indeed, none of them were in positions to do so, and interview evidence suggests that some of them would not have done so even if
they had been.[115] Second, support from members of the ruling
party, whether on the "backbenches" of the Lok Sabha or in high
places [116] or as customers in the clandestine trade in "pure gold"
ornaments, even more than support from opposition politicians, encouraged the associations in the gold trade to persist in their fights
against the rules.

Opposition among Congressmen was widely noted: by G. B.
Kotak, by the special Congress By-elections Committee formed in
1963, by journalists,[117] and by the informal group of officials who
advised the Finance Ministry. It manifested itself on the floor of Parliament, in the joint committee, in the Congress Parliamentary
party,[118] in the AICC, in Pradesh committees, and in testimony
given by Congressmen in connection with the loss of the Farrukhabad, Amroha, and Rajkot "prestige" by-elections. It has been suggested that dissenting-but-disciplined Congressmen acted as authenticators of oppositional messages from outside the Congress

114. Letter, 3 December 1968.
115. B. L. Chandak, M.P., New Delhi, 25 October 1966.
116. For example, the honorary secretary of the Jewellers Association regarded Manubhai Shah, then a minister of state, as the jewelers' friend in
court, and the president of India as "sympathetic"; interview.
117. For example, Inder Malhotra, in an article favoring the establishment of
gold control as a permanent policy, wrote that Congress "has not even paid
gold control the kind of lip service it did to . . . the law against untouchabil-
ity"; *Statesman*, 7 July 1963.
118. *Hindu*, 6 March 1963, and *Pioneer*, 19 December 1964.

"system" for a divided Congress-Government elite. Particularly striking in this case was the availability and autonomy of the Congress organization as a channel of communication for these messages. By lending their support to what by 1966 had become a general demand that at least the "quality control" provision of the rules be lifted, these Congressmen validated the general economic judgment that the rules were not accomplishing what they were meant to accomplish and were not likely to do so, and the general normative judgments that democratic political parties ought not to ignore the sentiments of their members or deprive thousands of innocent men of their livelihoods as a means of economic development.

The Congress-Government elites' patterns of decision making in this case are strikingly similar to the patterns they followed in the case of Bombay reorganization. There is the same pattern of decision making based upon "objective" state- and nation-building criteria and exaggerated notions of the leadership capabilities of Congress hierarchs, the same reliance on "experts" for advice and legitimation, the same failure to come to grips with particular interests until the battle was joined, and the same unwillingness to bring into the formal negotiating process people other than Congressmen.

There was no consultation with the gold trade before Morarji Desai's announcement of the rules on 9 January 1963. One might argue that such consultation would have been difficult if not impossible because, with the exception of the "top class of jewelers," the trade was not organized before then. This, however, was not Morarji Desai's argument. Fundamentally, the trade was not consulted because Desai and his colleagues did not think it had any legitimate right to be consulted. Lack of organization in the trade merely facilitated the government's right not to consult it. Morarji Desai is unmistakably clear on this point: the interests of the nation, as its leaders conceive it, come first, and the dislocation of any particular groups, especially groups which the finance minister held in as low esteem as those in the gold trade, is no argument against a policy in the national interest. "I know that a large number of people abuse me for this policy but I do not mind as long as I am sure my policy is correct." By way of analogy: prohibition cannot be abandoned because it dislocates the distillers.[119] Mrs. Sinha questions the propriety of consulting "interested parties" and asks mockingly how it

119. Interview, and *Hindustan Times*, 25 February 1963.

would have been possible to consult every woman in India who wears gold! [120]

Lest it be thought that this attitude toward consultation was peculiar to Mr. Desai and his deputy minister, it should be recalled that Krishnamachari's "fourteen-carat concession" came as a surprise to the smiths, although by that time the Akhil Bharatiya Swarnakar Sangh was organized. There was no consultation with the trade on the Gold (Control) Bill before it was introduced in Parliament, although by that time the All-India Sarafa Association had also been organized.

There were a great many "consultations" after the rules were announced between spokesmen for the gold trade and politicians and officials in the Finance Ministry and on the Gold Control Board. But these were not consultations on possible revisions in the rules which would incorporate in some fashion, shaped by bargaining and compromise, the goals of gold control and the interests of the trade. One did not intrinsically exclude the other. Nor were representatives of the gold trade opposed to all the goals of gold control and uncompromising in their demand for a return to the status quo ante. The Swarnakar Sangh's suggestion for reorganizing the trade as *swarna-slipa*, for example, was on its face no less valid an approach to smuggling and its related problems that "quality control." And it seems unlikely that some variation of *swarna-silpa* or a similar plan could not have been worked out that would have been acceptable to the *sarafs*. G. B. Kotak, the first chairman of the Gold Control Board, came to believe that the Swarnakar Sangh's suggestion that the government import gold and make it available for ornament manufacture, part of the *swarna-silpa* demand, was a good one.[121] But the Finance Ministry's position was that the gold control scenario was not negotiable. Morarji Desai reported that he met with spokesmen for the gold trade several times after the rules were promulgated. But he would not accept any of their suggestions because they conflicted with the ministry's plans for a phased tightening of its vise on gold consumption.[122]

The Swarnakar Sangh noted that "We . . . have time and again sat round the table with the President, the Prime Minister, the Fi-

120. Interview.
121. Interview.
122. Interview.

nance Minister, the Chief Ministers, some Members of Parliament and State Legislatures and have each and every time placed our contentions before their 'courts.' . . . [But] there has so far been no move whatsoever to modify the measure." [123]

At best sessions such as these produced only palliatives and mollifications, concessions on such peripheral matters as license fees, number of employees, record keeping, and so forth. For example, Krishnamachari reported to the Lok Sabha that he had met with a group of *sarafs*, and that they had requested the following. (1) That the "fourteen-carat concession" be extended to them. (2) That they should be permitted to sell old ornaments of "pure gold." (3) That the government should make bullion available to dealers. (4) That the sale of jewelry and the lending of money should be permitted on the same premises. (5) That assistance and in some cases compensation should be extended to dealers who were put out of business by the rules. (6) That the license fee for dealers should be reduced. The government, said its finance minister, had rejected all these requests but the last. The license fee was reduced from one hundred rupees to twenty-five rupees.[124]

In this case as in the other, the Congress leadership was unwilling to involve in decision making not only interest associations, but theoretically autonomous parliamentary structures as well. And in this case it would have been expedient to do so. As experienced an M.P. and senior Congressman as Panjabrao Deshmukh [125] guessed aloud that the government's reason for referring the Gold (Control) Bill to a joint committee was to have it killed there. The government's decision, he said, was "a sound one, namely not taking the responsibility for killing [the rules] but leaving it to the chosen representatives of the two houses to do the job." [126] There is little doubt that the joint committee would have done the job had it not been for the presence of the Congress whip on the committee in the persons of Krishnamachari and a former deputy minister of finance under Morarji Desai, B. R. Bhagat. "Whip" is perhaps too strong a term; "influence" might be more apt. Nine Congressmen did dissent from the committee's report, but it is clear from the evidence published

123. Akhil Bharatiya Swarnakar Sangh, *Whither Gold Control?*
124. *Lok Sabha Debates*, 3d series, vol. 23, 13 February 1964.
125. A former Union minister of agriculture and president of the Vidarbha PCC.
126. *Lok Sabha Debates*, 3rd series, vol. 32, 4 June 1964.

by the committee [127] that the sentiments expressed in their minute were the sentiments of the majority of Congressmen on the committee. There is no doubt that the government representatives on the committee made clear to their Congress colleagues that they were expected to support the bill.[128]

In addition to hearing testimony from forty-seven associations, almost all of them in the gold trade and unanimous in their opposition to the rules and the bill, the joint committee received about two hundred thousand written representation. Most of these, according to an Independent member of the committee, contained "outpourings of disapprobation . . . for gold control." [129] A Congress member of the joint committee, who was critical of the bill but did not sign her colleagues' minute of dissent, was later to remark of all this evidence, "I was simply astonished to see the number of representations against the Bill. . . . It is not very easy to throw all these things into the dustbin." [130] That, however, was where they were thrown.

On at least two publicized occasions the government turned to committees of "expert" officials for advice and legitimation. One committee, headed by S. S. Khera, reported before the introduction of the Gold (Control) Bill in Parliament; the other, headed by the secretary in the Union Ministry of Home Affairs, L. P. Singh, gave its report in September 1966. No attempt was made to bring the "experts" and the gold trade together to work out a mutually acceptable, compromise gold control formula. The Akhil Bharatiya Swarnakar Sangh's demand that "there should be a representation of goldsmiths, artisans, and workers on the Gold Control Board" was ignored.[131] The Khera Committee, by its own admission, did not even talk to spokesmen for the trade.[132] Both committees supported the gold control scenario. The Khera Committee regarded the "fourteen-carat concession" of the minister to whom it reported as a "purely political" step, a "transitional though decidedly retrograde measure." [133] The L. P. Singh Committee reported that "no

127. India, Lok Sabha Secretariat, *Joint Committee on the Gold (Control) Bill of 1963: Evidence* (September 1964).
128. Interviews.
129. L. M. Singhvi in India, Lok Sabha Secretariat, *Joint Committee . . . : Evidence.* Not all of these documents were available to me.
130. Nandani Satpathy in *Rajya Sabha Debates*, vol. 53, 30 August 1965.
131. Akhil Bharatiya Swarnakar Sangh, *Whither Gold Control?*
132. India, Lok Sabha Secretariat, *Joint Committee . . . : Evidence.*
133. *Hindu*, 5 December 1963.

economic or financial development" warranted a change in the government's policy.

Ironically, Mrs. Gandhi read the L. P. Singh Committee's recommendations to the Lok Sabha as part of her announcement that the government was abandoning "quality control." Because of "centuries old traditions and customs," she said, "all the restrictions on making gold ornaments of more than fourteen carats . . . will be withdrawn." [134] In sum, eventually coming to grips with the opposition that it had tried to ignore, but which it could not ignore, the Congress-Government elite was compelled to throw into the dustbin its policy and the recommendations of its "experts" along with the representations of the gold trade. K. Hanumanthaya, a Congress M.P., responded to Mrs. Gandhi's announcement with a scorn that was certainly not absent from the feelings of many of his colleagues: "The opinion of members of Parliament was disregarded; the opinion in the country was disregarded. . . . They [the government] only wanted to consult a few officials." [135]

At one point early in the gold control controversy, Morarji Desai warned that "to tell the goldsmiths that all they need is to agitate will merely confuse the issue, delay the resettlement, and help nobody at all." [136] If his caution fell on deaf ears, he and his colleagues and successors share no small part of the blame. When the smiths and *sarafs* pressed their demands within the parliamentary framework, they and their spokesmen were ignored, rebuffed, or subjected to fiat. Even the "fourteen-carat concession," in many ways the turning point in this case, was not something for which the goldsmiths had bargained. It was a "concession." And since they hadn't bargained for it they saw it as a product of their agitation.[137] In similar fashion, Mrs. Gandhi's announcement of the government's abandonment of "quality control" in September 1966, six months after such a step had been recommended by the Congress Working Committee and three months after the Bombay meeting of the AICC, came while thousands of goldsmiths were demonstrating in the streets outside Parliament House and their leader was on an "in-

134. *Lok Sabha Debates,* 2 September 1966, mimeographed.
135. Ibid., 3 September 1966.
136. *Hindu,* 11 July 1963.
137. Resolution of the Salem session of the general council of the ABSS, August 1965, in Hindi.

definite" fast. No new arguments against the rules were raised in the Lok Sabha in September that had not been made many times before, no new data was available that was not available when the smiths and *sarafs* pleaded their case before the joint committee two years earlier. If those nascent democrats, the smiths, were to conclude that in a democracy arguments are heard most clearly when they are raised outside Parliament House, it should come as no surprise to those within.

6 CONCLUSION

The burdens of national reconstruction fall squarely on the political system in a developing nation-state. However useful they may be to mass mobilization and elite recruitment, the politics of who gets what, when, and how will not suffice for India. Indian politics, if they are to be productive, cannot be limited to tussles between political luminaries and local and regional, caste and communal, economic and political factions over prestige, positions, and scarce resources. There is simply too much that cries to be done. But because only limited political capabilities are available to confront vast problems and only an underdeveloped associational infrastructure is extant to provide political information about them, government also bears the burden of husbanding its capabilities carefully and committing them prudently. If there is any lesson here, it may be, as Bismarck observed, to adjust one's appetite to the state of one's teeth. Or to know what to eat and what to leave. A cabinet of middle-aged to elderly Indian politicians might have known that the Gold Control Rules would never work, if for no other reason than that they have wives and daughters and daughters-in-law. Now, ten years after the creation of Maharashtra and Gujarat, it seems that much of the controversy and conflict over Bombay reorganization was unnecessary and wasteful. "The most dangerous decades" may see neither the disintegration of the Indian Union on linguistic-provincial lines or its adoption of an authoritarian regime.[1] But it is unlikely that they have passed.

Although the jobs of state- and nation-building must be approached with discretion as well as zeal (and the latter has not always been present either), there is no inclination here to minimize

1. Ten years ago these seemed to be the possible alternatives to Selig S. Harrison in his pioneering study of the centrifugal pulls on Indian nationhood of the combination of linguistic-provincial and caste loyalties; *India: The Most Dangerous Decades* (Princeton, N.J.: Princeton University Press, 1960).

151

them — or their risks. The shapes of Indian political arenas are amorphous, and the identities, strategies, capabilities, and even the existence of all the potential contestants may be unknown until a particular battle is joined. The structuring force of policy on politics is by no means unique to India or to new states. No one who has observed the impact of the Vietnam war on America's domestic politics, for example, would be inclined to argue this. But surely there is a difference in degree.

India's "public philosophy" cannot be "interest group liberalism." [2] In relative terms, the great constellations of organized interests with whom government can work out public policy do not exist at the national level of Indian politics. There is certainly some validity to the argument that before the advent of the Gold Control Rules there were no organizations in the gold trade — a large and ancient industry — with whom the Finance Ministry might have worked things out. The contestants were called forth by the battle, and after their victory, as in the case of Bombay reorganization, they dispersed. Whether the government would have attempted to work things out in advance with associations in the gold trade had they existed is another question and, of course, an unanswerable one. However, at least in this case, "paternalistic liberalism" seemed to be the government's "public philosophy" not merely by default but by preference.

The cases here suggest not only the complexity of India's emergent associational infrastructure but also the role played by policy in shaping it. The linguistic-provincial associations in western India and the associations in the gold trade were built, in part, on the foundations of preexisting secondary organizations with more homogeneous memberships and more diffuse demands. In both cases, not only were these associations formed in response to Congress-Government policies, but their internal and external relationships responded to these policies. Opposition to the Congress-Government formulas for Bombay reorganization and the Gold Control Rules engaged regional, caste, class, and political interests which in some instances reinforced each other, as among the Brahman lawyers of Nagpur; in some instances heightened existing tensions, as between goldsmith-*swarnakars* and goldsmith-*sarafs*; in some in-

2. For a discussion of this in the United States see Theodore Lowi, "The Public Philosophy: Interest Group Liberalism," *American Political Science Review*, vol. 65, March 1967.

stances created fissures in old relationships, as between the scheduled caste RPI of Maharashtra and the scheduled caste RPI of Nag-Vidarbha; in some instances brought old antagonists into new formations or papered over old antagonisms, as the Praja Socialists and Communists in Maharashtra and the *bhujan samaj* and Brahmans in Nagpur, and so forth.

These responses were for the most part intermittent and short-lived. But so were the policies. We may anticipate that the associational infrastructure and the capabilities of the political system for sustained penetration of its environment will develop, if at all, together. And until these developments occur,[3] there is no reason to suppose that opposition will not continue to be cued by particular ruling party (or parties)-government policies and that it will not continue to take the form of ad hoc and transient supportive relationships among interested groups. There is also no reason to assume that whoever inherits the Delhi *gaddi* within the near future will inherit with it any greater capabilities to affect or control its environment than Congress's. Events since the fourth general elections suggest that these capabilities may indeed be reduced with the passing of the old order.

One additional observation. Although it is undoubtedly true that as Indians have become more and more politically mobilized some loci of political power have shifted from towns and cities to the countryside, the importance of urban centers and urban leadership in the formation and direction of secondary associations in the cases here should be noted. No doubt this may be attributed, in part, to the peculiarities of the cases. But it may be that as secondary associations develop in scale and complexity, the human and material resources of cities and their seats of political authority become more salient to them. Take the relationship between the Samyukta Maharashtra Samiti and Bombay city as an example, perhaps an extreme one. The leaders of the samiti saw the city as a paracolonial enclave which exploited the resources of its Maharashtrian hinterland. Their appeal to the Marhattas in the hinterland, on whom the samiti's electoral strength depended, was that by making Bombay

3. Following Samuel P. Huntington and Lucien Pye, Rajni Kothari contrasts "modernization" — processes such as participation and mobilization, and "development" — the institutionalization of these processes into a "stable and legitimized polity"; "Tradition and Modernity Revisited," *Government and Opposition*, vol. 3, Summer 1968.

city the capital of Maharashtra the pattern of exploitation would be reversed.

"One-party dominance" was used with some reservation in these studies because as a descriptive term its usefulness seemed limited. In this regard, it is important to note the qualifications that Professors Kothari and Morris-Jones attach to "one-party dominance," for there is certainly a risk that in the unqualified use of such terms political science may be using the "behavorial persuasion" to adopt a new formalism after having rejected an older one.

Kothari notes that "the sensitivity of the entire [Indian political] system depends on the sensitivity of the *margin of pressure*, its flexibility and general responsiveness being a function of the elbow room it provides to factions, dissident groups, and opposition parties in the making of critical choices and decisions." [4]

Morris-Jones finds that the interaction between movements inside and outside Congress "constitutes the core of Indian political life."

Tensions and factions within Congress stimulate and are stimulated by the pressures of outside groups. The latter operate currently by weaning away the disillusioned elements and partly by giving confidence and encouragement to those of their way of thought who stay within the ample folds of the Congress.[5]

In these studies "one-party dominance" was partially descriptive of a relationship within the political system, but it did not describe, even when Congress was clearly "dominant," the relationship between the system and its environment. This was the source of the paradox with which these studies began. Even at the height of its power, supported by overwhelming majorities in Parliament and the legislative assemblies and led by a prime minister–party president without peer or competitor, the national Congress-Government elite could not reorganize Bombay as it wished. Nor could it, a few years later, effectively control the domestic consumption and saving of gold.

Even as it applied to the political system, "one-party dominance" was a term of limited descriptiveness. That is, aside from those areas in India where it was clearly inapplicable, Kerala, for example, even

4. Rajni Kothari, "The Congress 'System' in India," *Asian Survey* 4 (December 1964): 1164–73.
5. W. H. Morris-Jones, *The Government and Politics of India* (London: Hutchinson and Co., 1964).

where it formally applied, as it did in Bombay between 1956 and
1960, it was a "dominance" based upon compromise among party
leaders whose institutional positions exaggerated their leadership
capabilities and whose agreements reflected their inability to control the political situation. Ironically, the pursuit by Congress hierarchs of "dominance" as a goal in itself within the framework of a
democratic political system probably reduced their willingness to
brave opposition in the pursuit of other state- and nation-building
goals.

A concept related to "one-party dominance" and also of limited
usefulness was that of Congress as a "system." It was at best a
loosely articulated system. Its boundaries were nebulous and the
roles which formed its interrelated parts were not all played by
Congressmen. It is difficult not to conclude from these studies that
Congressmen and opposition politicians operated within the same
system. In the case of Bombay reorganization, the more important
decisions made by Congress party leaders were in no small measure
dependent on inputs from the opposition, although formal authoritative negotiations were closed to it. Congress dissidents operated
at the boundaries of the Congress "system" and they were effective
not because they worked within it but because they threatened it
from outside where they could attach their strength to the strength
of opposition coalitions.

With the passing of "one-party dominance" and perhaps of the
"one party" itself, critical reevaluations of their nature will certainly
be made. It may well be that what political scientists have been describing was a "one-party dominant" *situation* in a political system
that is still very much in the stages of development.[6] But whether
"one-party dominance" is viewed as a situation or as a system, its
importance to Indian political development may yet to have its
most dramatic demonstration. The pursuit of "dominance" by Congress leaders, however chimerical, suggests a characteristic (the distinctive characteristic?) of their party that from most present indica-
tions is unlikely to be replicated in its coalition successors: a capa-
bility and a willingness born of necessity to aggregate into policy
alternatives a broad and diverse range of interests. The Congress
leaders who negotiated and renegotiated a settlement of the Bombay reorganization question were hardly without factional affiliations — many were faction leaders — but they shared an affilia-

6. I am indebted to Professor Iqbal Narain for this suggestion.

tion with one organization and a stake in its retention of power. Compare the fruits of their labors with those of the Samyukta Maharashtra Samiti and the Mahagujarat Janata Parishad!

With the loss of Congress "dominance" and the opening of other avenues to political power, the compulsion to aggregate broadly is reduced for faction leaders, and groups interested in political power may more readily turn to parties other than Congress. It becomes possible for oppositional inputs to force changes in political personnel and parties, but whether or not this will increase the system's aggregative capabilities remains to be seen. Edward Shils's general observation seems quite applicable to the political situation in India since the fourth general elections:

> The prospect of disintegration [of the dominant party] encourages the opposition parties outside the government, but it does not "civilize" them. It only excites them. The small and ineffective opposition parties of the time are not made stronger or more reasonable by the imminence of the breakup of the congress-like ruling party.[7]

These studies suggest that there is considerable political vitality in Indian society. They contribute additional evidence of the capacity of primordial and small secondary groups to adopt the roles of interest associations and federations and thus to mediate between the traditional and modern "idioms" of Indian politics and give life and substance to India's democratic constitution.

This capacity for "organized pluralism" has been a source of optimism for friends of Indian democracy. But there is enough disturbing evidence and a sufficient number of warning voices to temper this optimism with caution. It is generally agreed that after twenty-two years the benefits of democracy and development have gone disproportionately to those Indians, rural and urban, who had something to begin with, whereas the vast underlying population who had little or nothing now has little or nothing more.[8] It might be instructive to compare the benefits gained by the peasant-proprietor Marathas from their participation in the creation of Maharashtra with those of the landless laborer scheduled castes from theirs.

To be sure, "organized pluralism" in India can be and has been a means for redistributing benefits. The Maharashtrian Brahmans are

7. Edward Shils, "Opposition in the New States of Asia and Africa," ibid., vol. 1, January 1966.
8. For example, see *Seminar*, no. 121, September 1969, devoted to a discussion of the Congress party.

aware of this. But it is certainly a means with limits. Robert Dahl, writing about Western democracies, cites two problems of "organized pluralism" that have "not been solved anywhere."

For one thing since all resources except the vote are unequally distributed some minorities (one thinks of the uneducated poor in the United States) may not have much in the way of political resources to bargain with: they have the ballot and little else. In addition, to the extent that parliament is excluded from the process and elections provide only a vague and uncertain control over national leaders, there is no political institution in which majorities weigh heavily that can control the great bargained decisions by means of public review, appraisal, opposition, amendment, or veto.[9]

These problems, serious enough in the West, are perhaps even more pressing in India, where resources are more unequally distributed, organized interests fewer, the population excluded from bargained decisions larger, and the domain of politics more restricted and autonomous of social life. It is really an open question whether the major thrust of "organized pluralism" in the foreseeable Indian future will be to continue to redistribute benefits among those strata of the population who are already relatively privileged and to create new benefits for them or to bring into the developing polity and economy substantial sections of the poor and the despised.

Some years ago, Barrington Moore, Jr., observed that

Some students of Indian affairs have expressed surprise that India's small Western-educated elite has remained faithful to the democratic ideal when they could so easily overthrow it. But why would they wish to overthrow it? Does not democracy provide a rationalization for refusing to overhaul a social structure that maintains their privileges?[10]

The significance of Moore's observation today is twofold: it contains the germ of an important truth and it is dated. The important truth is that "organized pluralism" may be used as an efficient instrument by the privileged to maintain and legitimate their privileges and to deny them to the less fortunate – all in the name of democracy. But democracy in India is no longer a thing of the "Western-educated elite," and the day when they as a class could "so easily overthrow it" has undoubtedly passed. Democratic politics have compelled them to share power with new men and they

9. Robert Dahl, "Reflections on Opposition in Western Democracies," *Government and Opposition*, vol. 1, October 1965.
10. Barrington Moore, Jr., *Social Origins of Dictatorship and Democracy* (Boston: Beacon Press, 1966), p. 431.

have been losing their capacity for monopolistic self-perpetuation as higher education, for example, falls more and more under the influence of democratic politics. In some measure this is what anti-Brahmanism in Maharashtra is about.

Democracy and "organized pluralism" do provide means for narrowing the gap between politics and life, and for some very ordinary Indians that gap is certainly narrowing. If cautious and critical evaluations of the performance of democracy in India are in order, despairing ones seem unwarranted or at least premature. The *swarnakars*, for example, were perfectly ordinary, relatively nonpoliticized people, not of the most deprived social order but certainly not of the most privileged. They were ordinary enough to have their vital interests dismissed quite casually. But they clung tenaciously to them and with their own leaders and widespread support they met authority on its own ground and successfully opposed it.

Successful opposition reveals as perhaps nothing else can a middle course between sheepish submission to the will of authority or parochial rejection of it, on the one side, and threatening the system and risking one's all to destroy authority on the other. Opposition is one of democracy's schools and "revolutions are the symptoms of the failure of opposition, not of its success." [11] In the long run, the *swarnakars'* victory and victories like theirs may prove to have been more functional for the democratic system than its realization of some gold control scenario.

If opposition in India is not yet "responsible," it nonetheless performs the vital function of checking authority, and its lack of responsibility should be measured against the gap between politics and life — not only Congress politics but opposition politics as well. Bertrand de Journevel, in discussing the Roman tribunate, notes that its "essential value . . . was that the people were defended by those who did not aspire to become masters." [12] The *swarnakars*, it might be remembered, in their unwillingness to place their defense entirely in the hands of opposition politicians, instinctively grasped this point.

The democrat will have no difficulty in evaluating Congress's performance in the two cases here as something less than perfect. It

11. Leonard Shapiro, "Foreword," *Government and Opposition*, vol. 1, October 1965.
12. Bertrand de Journevel, "The Means of Contestation," ibid., January 1966.

overestimated its own capabilities and underestimated the capabilities of its opponents, and because it did so it was forced to retreat on policies that its leaders had declared to be of major state- and nation-building importance. It attempted to close its "system" to pressures from outside and recognized their validity only when it was compelled to by its own fears and failures and by threats of violence and embarrassment. It tampered with the parliamentary system in order to maintain its "dominance." It used "expert" opinions to justify its policies, but discarded these opinions when they became political liabilities.

Yet to cite Congress's obvious shortcomings in this fashion is to fall into the common case-study errors of describing the trees without regard to the forest and measuring performance against absolute rather than relative standards. Congress has no doubt played the democratic game to its advantage, at times clumsily, at times shortsightedly, and at times by cutting corners. But it has played it. The 1957 elections in Maharashtra were not postponed, nor were their results declared null and void. S. A. Dange and S. M. Joshi were not placed under "preventive detention" before the elections and the candidacies of Samyukta Maharashtra Samiti politicians were not declared invalid. No attempt was made to confiscate gold at its international price, nor were goldsmiths "resettled," nor were Congress hierarchs ultimately insensitive to demands that they behave democratically and humanely.

In sum, Congress has not so much restricted democratic opposition as "one-party dominance" has structured its flow. Some of this structuring will undoubtedly change as "one-party dominance" fades, but it is at least possible that because groups like the Akhil Bharatiya Swaranakar Sangh and the Samyukta Maharashtra Samiti have demonstrated its efficacy, the generally democratic direction of opposition will continue. Whether Congress hierarchs contributed to the establishment of a democratic process of opposition because they feared the consequences of not doing so,[13] or out of genuine ideological commitment to democratic processes, or, more likely, out of a combination of both is perhaps less important than the con-

13. Robert Dahl observes that formal opposition is likely to be tolerated if (a) the government believes that attempts to coerce opposition would be likely to fail or (b) even if the attempt were to succeed, the costs of coercion would exceed the gain. Political Opposition in Western Democracies, chap. 1; quoted by Hans Daalder, "Government and Opposition in New States," ibid.

tribution itself. One need only scan the list of constitutions that have been discarded since 1950, martial law and one-party systems established, legislatures prorogued, political parties and associations banned, and revolutions and coups d'etat to gain some measure of the contribution's worth and Congress's judiciousness in making it when, during the heyday of "one-party dominance," it was confronted with a maximum of temptation and what appeared deceptively to be a minimum of restraint.

Bibliography

INTERVIEWS AND NEWSPAPER REPORTS

A substantial amount of information that is contained in these studies was obtained from interview evidence. Approximately one hundred interviews were held in various parts of India during the year 1966–67. In most instances interviewees and the dates and places of the interviews are identified in footnotes or in the text. In a few instances interviewees asked not to be identified by name, and in a few more I judged it either prudent or considerate not to identify them.

English-language dailies were another important source of information. For the most part this information was culled from the great volume of newspaper reports that are carefully collected and cataloged by the Press Information Section of the All-India Congress Committee in New Delhi. The newspapers that were relied upon most heavily are: *Amrita Bazar Patrika, Bombay Chronicle, Deccan Herald, Express, Free Press Journal, Hindu, Hindustan Standard, Hindustan Times, Hitavada, National Herald, Patriot, Pioneer, Statesman,* and *Tribune.*

OFFICIAL PUBLICATIONS

The Reorganization of Bombay

Bombay. *Legislative Assembly Debates,* vol. 10, pt. 2 (14, 16 March 1960).
Bombay. Ministry of Law. *The Bombay Tenancy and Agricultural Land (Vidarbha Region and Kutch Area) (Amendment) Act of 1962.*
———. *Report of the Commission of Inquiry (Shri Justice S. P. Kotval) on the Cases of Police Firing at Ahmadabad on the 12th, 13th, and 14th August 1958.*
Constituent Assembly of India. *Report of the Linguistic Provinces Commission.* 1948.
India. *Census of India 1921,* vol. 8, pt. 2, Bombay Presidency.
India. *Lok Sabha Debates.* Vol. 10, pt. 2 (14–23 December 1955); vol. 4, pt. 2 (18, 23 April 1956); vol. 6, pt. 2 (26, 30, 31 July and 2 August 1956); vol. 7, pt. 2 (7, 9 August 1956); vol. 6, pt. 2 (25 July 1959); 2d ser., vol. 41 (28, 31 March and 1 April 1960); 2d ser., vol. 43 (14 April 1960).

India, Census Commission. *Census of India 1951*. Paper no. 1, Languages-1951 Census, Dangs District.
———. *Census of India 1961*. Vol. 5 Gujarat, pt. 10-C, Special Migrant Tables for Ahmadabad City; vol. 10 Maharashtra, pt. 1-B Greater Bombay Census Tables, pt. 1-C Greater Bombay Special Migration Tables, pt. 5-A; District Census Handbook 17, Dangs District.
India, Election Commission. *Report on the First General Elections in India, 1952*, vol. 2 Statistical.
———. *Report on the Second General Elections in India, 1957*. Vol. 2. Statistical.
———. *Report on the Third General Elections in India, 1962*. Vol. 2 Statistical.
———. *Results of Byelections Held between April 1957 and March 1959*.
———. *Results of Byelections Held between April 1959 and May 1960*.
India, Ministry of Law. *Bombay Reorganization Act of 1960*.
———. *States Reorganization Act of 1956*.
India, States Reorganization Commission. *Report, 1955*.

Gold Control

India. *Lok Sabha Debates*. 3d ser., vol. 12 (20, 21 February 1963); vol. 14 (5, 6, 7 March 1963); vol. 16 (11 April 1963); vol. 19 (22, 29 August 1963); vol. 21 (12, 19, 21 September 1963); vol. 23 (5 December 1963); vol. 25 (13 February 1964); vol. 32 (4, 5 June 1964); vol. 33 (10 September 1964); vol. 37 (21, 22, 23, 24 December 1964); vol. 55 (5 May 1966); 23 August and 2, 3 September 1966, mimeographed.
India. *Rajya Sabha Debates*. Vol. 53 (30 August 1965).
India, Election Commission. *Results of Byelections Held between August 1961 and June 1963*.
India, Lok Sabha Secretariat. *The Gold (Control) Bill of 1963; Report of the Joint Committee*, September 1964.
———. *Joint Committee on the Gold (Control) Bill of 1963; Evidence*. September 1964.
India, Ministry of Law. *Defence of India Act of 1962*.
———. *Gold Control Act of 1964*.
———. *Rules under the Defense of India Act of 1962*. 2d ed., 1965.

ASSOCIATION AND PARTY PUBLICATIONS

Reorganization of Bombay

All-India Congress Committee. *The General Elections of 1957: A Survey*. New Delhi, 1959.
All Parties Conference, 1928. *Report of the Committee Appointed by the Conference to Determine the Principles of the Constitution for India*. All-India Congress Committee, 1928.

Aney, Madhao Shrihari. *Memorandum Submitted to the States Reorganization Commission.* Yeotmal; Yeotmal District Association, n.d.

Bombay Citizens' Committee. *Memorandum Submitted to the States Reorganization Commission.* Bombay, 1964.

Communist Party of India. *New Age,* 1, 22 November 1959.

Deshmukh, G. V. *Maharashtra Unification Conference.* Bombay 1948.

Divatia, H. V. *Memorandum to the States Reorganization Commission.* Bombay: Gujarat Sahitya Parishad. 1954.

Gadgil, D. R. *The Future of Bombay City.* Bombay: Samyukta Maharashtra Parishad, n.d.

Gujarat Pradesh Congress Committee and Gujarat Sima Samiti. *Memorandum Submitted to the States Reorganization Commission.* Ahmadabad, 1954.

Indian Merchants' Chamber. *Diamond Jubilee Souvenir.* Bombay 1967.

Indian National Congress. *Congress Bulletin.* 24 January 1946; February–March 1954; May 1954; June–July 1954; January 1956; March 1956; October–November 1958.

————. *Report of the Linguistic Provinces Committee Appointed by the Jaipur Congress.* New Delhi: Indian National Congress, 1949.

————. *Report of the Thirty-fifth Session of the Indian National Congress held at Nagpur on the 26th, 28th, and 31st December 1920.* Nagpur 1920.

————. *Resolutions on States Reorganization, 1920–1956.*

Mahagujarat Parishad. *Formation of Mahagujarat: A Memorandum Submitted to the States Reorganization Commission.* Vallabh Vidyanagar, 1954.

Praja Socialist Party. *Report of the Third National Conference.* Bangalaore, 25–28 November 1956.

————. *Report of the Fourth National Conference.* Poona, 25–28 May 1958.

————. *Report of the Fifth National Conference.* Bombay, 5–9 November 1959.

Samyukta Maharashtra Parishad. *Reorganization of States in India with Particular Reference to the Formation of Maharashtra.* Bombay, 1954.

————. *United Maharashtra.* Bombay 1948.

Samyukta Maharashtra Parishad, Nag-Vidarbha Samiti. *Supplementary Memorandum Submitted to the States Reorganization Commission.*

Gold Control

Akhil Bharatiya Swarnakar Sangh. Miscellaneous printed and mimeographed pamphlets and notices in Hindi and English, generally untitled.

————. *Sadharan Parishad ke Salem Baithak ke Prastav* [Resolution of the Salem session of the general council]. August 1965.

————. "Supplementary Memorandum to the Joint Committee of Parliament on the Gold (Control) Bill of 1963." Mimeographed.

————. *Whither Gold Control?* Calcutta, n.d.

————, Bangiya [West Bengal] Swarna Silpa Samiti, Delhi Goldsmith

Workers Union, Gujarat Swarnakar Sangh, Madhya Pradesh Swarnakar Sangh, Maharashtra Pradesh Swarnakar Sangh, Rajasthan Sona Chandi Shrimik Sangh, and Tamilaha [Tamilnad] Viswakarma Central Sangham. Mimeographed memorandum submitted to the Joint Committee of Parliament on the Gold (Control) Bill of 1963.

All-Delhi Sarafa Association; All-India Sarafa Association; Andhra Pradesh Gold, Silver, and Diamond Merchants Association; Bullion Merchants Association of Delhi; Calcutta Gold and Silversmiths Association; Gold, Silver and Jawahrat Merchants Association of Indore; Gujarat State Gold Licensed Dealers Association; Madras Jewellers and Diamond Merchants Association; Navsari Chokshi Association; Shri Chokshi Mahajan, Ahmadabad; Shri Ratnapole and Richey Road Gold, Silver, and Jewellery Merchants Association of Ahmadabad; Shri Sarafa Committee of Agra; and Surat Chokshi Mahajan. Mimeographed memoranda submitted to the Joint Committee of Parliament on the Gold (Control) Bill of 1963.

All-India Congress Committee. *Byelections Committee Report*. Jaipur, 23 October 1963.

———. *Review of Byelection Results*. August 1963.

All-India Jewellers Association. "Repeal of Gold Control Order Meeting with Prime Minister Smt. Indira Gandhi." Mimeographed. 29 August 1966.

All-India Sarafa Association. *Facts on Gold Control*. Bombay, n.d.

———. *Gold Control in Retrospect*. Bombay, n.d.

———. *How Can Government Mobilize Gold for Defence*. Bombay, n.d.

Forum of Free Enterprise. *Report for the Year Ended July 30, 1966*, n.d.

Gem and Jewellery Export Promotion Council. *Memorandum and Articles of Incorporation*. 1966.

Goldsmith Workers Union, Delhi. Miscellaneous resolutions, petitions, and memoranda.

Indian National Congress. *Congress Bulletin*, April–June 1966.

Mahajan, B. S. *Rethinking on Gold Control*. Bombay: Forum of Free Enterprise, 1965.

Pethe, S. G. Speech delivered to a meeting of the Forum of Free Enterprise. 30 December 1966.

OTHER WORKS

General

Daalder, Hans. "Government and Opposition in New States." *Government and Opposition* 1 (January 1966).

Dahl, Robert. "Reflections on Opposition in Western Democracies." *Government and Opposition* 1 (October 1965).

Desai, Morarji. *In My View*. Bombay: Thacker and Co., 1966.

Erdman, Howard L. *The Swatantra Party and Indian Conservatism*. Cambridge: Cambridge University Press, 1967.

Hutton, J. H. *Caste in India*. 3d ed., London: Oxford Univ. Press, 1961.
Jena, B. B. *Parliamentary Committees in India*. Calcutta: Scientific Book Agency, 1966.
Journevel, Bertrand de. "The Means of Contestation." *Government and Opposition* 1 (January 1966).
Kochanek, Stanley A. *The Congress Party of India*. Princeton, N.J.: Princeton University Press, 1968.
Kothari, Rajni. "The Congress 'System' in India." *Asian Survey* 4 (December 1964): 1164–73.
———. "Tradition and Modernity Revisited." *Government and Opposition* 3 (Summer 1968).
Lelyveld, Joseph. "The Karma of Morarji Desai." *New York Times Magazine*, 24 September 1967.
Lowi, Theodore. "The Public Philosophy: Interest Group Liberalism." *American Political Science Review* 65 (March 1967).
Moore, Barrington, Jr. *Social Origins of Dictatorship and Democracy*. Boston: Beacon Press, 1966.
Morris-Jones, W. H. "Dominance and Dissent." *Government and Opposition* 1 (July–September 1966).
———. *The Government and Politics of India*. London: Hutchinson and Co., 1964.
———. *Parliament in India*. London: Longmans, Green and Co., 1957.
Overstreet, Gene D., and Windmiller, Marshall. *Communism in India*. Berkeley: University of California Press, 1960.
Pylee, M. V. *Constitutional Government in India*. Bombay: Asia Publishing House, 1960.
Rudolph, Lloyd I. "The Modernity of Tradition: The Democratic Incarnation of Caste in India." *American Political Science Review* 54 (December 1965).
Rudolph, Lloyd I., and Rudolph, Susanne H. "The Political Role of India's Caste Associations." *Pacific Affairs* 33 (March 1962).
Seminar. No. 121, September 1969.
Shapiro, Leonard. "Foreword." *Government and Opposition* 1 (October 1965).
Shils, Edward. "Opposition in the New States of Asia and Africa." *Government and Opposition* 1 (January 1966).
Shukla, V. N. *The Constitution of India*. 5th ed. Lucknow: Eastern Book Co., 1969.
Srinivas, M. N. *Social Change in Modern India*. Bombay: Allied Publishers, 1966.
Wallace, Paul. "India: The Dispersion of Political Power." *Asian Survey* 8 (February 1968).
Weiner, Myron. "Political Development in the Indian States." In *State Politics in India*, edited by Myron Weiner. Princeton, N.J.: Princeton University Press, 1968.
———. *The Politics of Scarcity*. Chicago: University of Chicago, 1962.

Reorganization of Bombay

Ambedkar, B. R. *Maharashtra as a Linguistic Province: A Statement Submitted to the Linguistic Provinces Commission.* Bombay: Thacker and Co., 1948.
————. *Thoughts on Linguistic States.* 1955.
Balasubramaniam, E. "Shiv Sena: Child of Congress." *Swarajya,* 27 May 1967.
Deogirikar, T. R. *Twelve Years in Parliament: Democracy in Action.* Poona: Chitrashala Prakashan, 1964.
Enlite, 1 April 1967.
Harrison, Selig S. *India: The Most Dangerous Decades.* Princeton, N.J.: Princeton University Press, 1960.
Indian Committee for Cultural Freedom. *Problems of Maharashtra.* Bombay, 1960.
Jack, Homer A., ed. *The Gandhi Reader.* Bloomington: Indiana University Press, 1956.
Kothari, Rajni, and Maru, Rushikesh. "Caste and Secularism in India." *Journal of Asian Studies* 25 (November 1965): 33–50.
Kulkarni, A. B. *The Second General Elections in Sholapur.* Sholapur: Institute of Public Administration, 1957.
Mukerji, K. P., and Ramaswami, S. *Reorganization of Indian States.* Bombay: Popular Book Depot, 1956.
Munshi, K. M. *Linguistic Provinces and the Future of Bombay.* Bombay, 1948.
Pathak, D. N., et al. *Three General Elections in Gujarat.* Ahmadabad: Gujarat University, 1966.
Patterson, Maureen L. P. "Caste and Political Leadership in Maharashtra." *Economic Weekly,* 25 September 1954.
Sharma, B. A. V. and Jangam, R. T. *The Bombay Municipal Corporation: An Election Study.* Bombay: Popular Book Depot, 1962.
Sirsikar, V. M. *Political Behaviour in India.* Bombay: Manaktalas, 1965.
Somjee, A. H. *Voting Behaviour in an Indian Village.* Baroda: Department of Political Science, M.S. University of Baroda, 1959.
Stern, Robert W. "Maharashtrian Linguistic-Provincialism and Indian Nationalism." *Pacific Affairs* 37 (Spring 1964).
Zelliot, Eleanor. "Buddhism and Politics in Maharashtra." In *South Asian Politics and Religion,* edited by Donald Eugene Smith. Princeton, N.J.: Princeton University Press, 1966.

Gold Control

Ahmed, Bashir, "Congress Defeat in Amroha." *Economic Weekly,* 22 May 1965.
Brij Bhushan, Jamila. *Indian Jewellery, Ornaments, and Decorative Designs.* Bombay: D. B. Taraporevala and Sons, 1964.
"Estimates of Gold and Silver Stocks in India." *Reserve Bank of India Bulletin* 12 (April 1958).

Gandhi, M. K. *Autobiography*. Ahmadabad: Navajivan Publishing House, 1927.

Hart, Henry C. Correspondence, 3 December 1968.

Institute of Constitutional and Parliamentary Studies. *Conparlist*, May and June–July 1969.

Marg: A Magazine of the Arts, September 1964.

Maru, Rushikesh. "Fall of a Traditional Congress Stronghold." *Economic Weekly*, 19 June 1965.

Narayanaswamy, S. "Gold and Common Sense." *Hindu*, 26 January 1963.

Ramayana. Translated by Shudha Mazumdar. Bombay: Bharatiya Vidya Bhavan, 1953.

Rangnekar, D. K. *Poverty and Capital Development in India*. London: Oxford University Press, 1959.

Roy, Rameshray. "Congress Defeat in Farrukhabad." *Economic Weekly*, 29 May 1965.

Shenoy, B. R. "Basic Factors of the Gold Problem." *Times of India*, 12 November 1964.

Srinivas, M. N. "Attachment to Gold." *Hitavada*, 26 February 1963.

Index

169